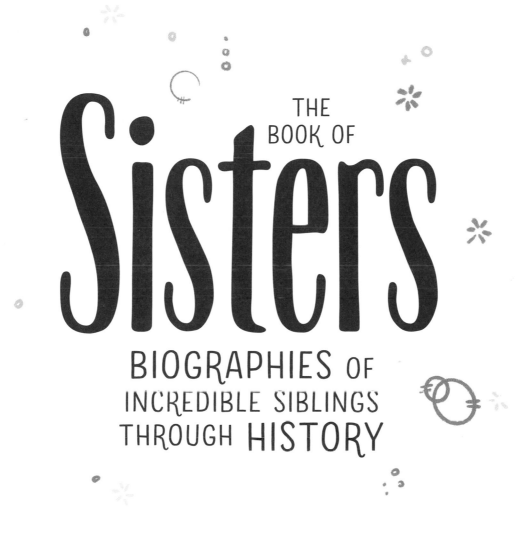

THE
BOOK OF

Sisters

BIOGRAPHIES OF
INCREDIBLE SIBLINGS
THROUGH HISTORY

NEON SQUID

CONTENTS

WHAT DOES IT MEAN TO BE A SISTER?

Sisters happen by chance. You can't choose your sister, or what she's like—yet it'll probably be the longest relationship in your life. People who study human cultures tell us sisterhood also tends to be our strongest, most life-changing connection.

Sisters often know each other's secrets—things even parents don't know. Your sister might like everything you like, or you could be total opposites; it's just the luck of the draw! Maybe that's what makes sisterhood so complicated. But it's also so powerful.

Sisters teach us to compete, to defend our territory, to lose, to stand up, to give in, to be vulnerable, to trust and betray, to dream.

> "WHAT OTHER KIND OF RELATIONSHIP IS SUCH A COMPLETE APPRENTICESHIP IN LOVE, CARE, AND WARFARE?"
>
> **SARAH WATLING**

A WORLD HISTORY THROUGH SISTERS

Knowing sisterhood is so powerful, we wondered: How have sisters changed the world? We decided to explore the whole history of the world through the stories of sisters. It's an unusual point of view but one that seems long overdue.

Writing this book, we discovered all kinds of sisters—sisters who loved and sisters who hated, sisters who helped each other achieve their dreams and sisters who held each other down. Even sisters who killed each other! These amazing stories prove it really is true: Across time and across the world, sisterhood has been a mighty force—of destruction, inspiration, and change.

A SPECIAL RELATIONSHIP

This book was especially fun for us, because we aren't just writing about sisters... we *are* sisters!

We're alike in many ways—we both travel the world, love Halloween, and have red hair. Sometimes, we're opposites: We have very different personalities and strongly disagree about celery. But like many of the sisters in this book, those differences have made us a great team.

KATIE AND OLIVIA

THE MOIRAI

THE ANCIENT GREEKS BELIEVED EVERY HUMAN'S LIFE WAS CONTROLLED BY THREE SISTERS

Humans just like us have lived and died on planet Earth for at least 200,000 years. And all that time, we've wondered why we are here, and what we should be doing. The ancient Greeks believed that our lives are controlled by three sisters—one young, one middle-aged, and one very old.

Every time Clotho, the youngest, spins a new thread on her spindle, a human—like you!—is born. The thread becomes your life. Next, Lachesis, the middle sister, measures the thread. She can make it as long or as short as she likes. That's how long your life will last. Finally, Atropos, who is called a "crone" because she is so old, cuts your string when it is your time to die. Atropos gets to decide how you die too. Gulp...

If you believed the Moirai controlled your whole destiny, would you live your life differently?

People have been telling the story of Clotho, Lachesis, and Atropos for thousands of years. It comes from a period called the Stone Age. We don't have much left from this time, except ancient stories like the legend of the Moirai, and hundreds of little stone statues. They are always of women!

HUMAN ORIGINS

Humans used to share Earth with many other humanlike species. But our brains are bigger than all the rest. That's probably why we survived and they didn't. We used our intelligence and creativity to tell stories, like this one, which helped us create bonds and form strong communities.

JEON JANGHWA & JEON HONGRYEON

SILENCE MAY HAVE COST THEM THEIR LIVES, BUT THESE SISTERS FINALLY SPOKE UP—AFTER THEIR DEATHS!

Once upon a time in Korea, legend tells of two sisters—Janghwa (Rose) and Hongryeon (Lotus). After their mother died, their father married again, not realizing his new wife was hateful and cruel. The sisters grew up, and soon Janghwa was engaged to be married. Their stepmother was angry about the fancy wedding—she wanted money to be spent on only her beloved sons. So she spread a terrible lie about Janghwa. When her father believed it, Janghwa ran crying into the forest. Her stepbrother followed her and drowned her in a pond.

Hongryeon was so upset about Janghwa's death, she also ran into the woods. Her body was found in the pond the next morning.

Years passed, and the village forgot about the sisters. But mysteriously, every new mayor who came to lead the town died the first night they arrived. Nobody understood why. Finally, a brave young mayor arrived, determined to solve the mystery. He sat awake all night, watching. Without warning, terrifying noises filled the air, his candle went out, and the door flew open. In the doorway hovered two ghosts—Janghwa and Hongryeon!

"We only want justice!" the sisters cried. Begging the mayor for help, they told him what their stepbrother had done. The next morning the mayor revealed the truth to the town, and the evil stepmother and her son were executed.

Many years later, the father saw his daughters in a dream. They told him they wanted to return to his family. Nine months later, the father's new wife gave birth to twin baby girls. They named them Janghwa and Hongryeon.

THE IMPORTANCE OF SPEECH

Speaking up was how the Jeon sisters finally found justice. Scientists think our ability to talk might be why early humans survived and thrived—we learned how to speak and share our knowledge with one another.

TILAFAIGA & TAEMA

BY SWIMMING ACROSS AN OCEAN, POLYNESIAN TWIN SISTERS LAUNCHED A NEW TRADITION

Long ago in Polynesia, in the heart of the Pacific Ocean, legend tells of sisters Taema and Tilafaiga. They were born conjoined, with their bodies connected at their backs. As they grew, the twins became famous for their courage and adventurous spirits. So when people in Fiji wanted to share their traditional *tatau* (tattoo) with others, they asked Tilafaiga and Taema. The sisters were sent to teach people in Samoa how to create complex designs on skin using sharpened bones and ink. They also learned one important rule: Tattoos were only for women!

The twins began the 700-mile (1,100-km) swim to Samoa, singing "tattoo the women, not the men" over and over as they swam. But along the way, they spotted a beautiful clam on the ocean floor. They dived down to catch it. Just then, a powerful wave smashed into the sisters, pulling them under and breaking their bodies apart. They swam frantically, not sure if they'd ever make it back to the surface alive. When they finally reached air, they stared at each other in wonder. Taema and Tilafaiga had never seen one another's faces before!

They began to swim again, side by side. But in all the chaos, the sisters' song had become confused. Now they sang "tattoo the men, not the women." When they arrived in Samoa, they delivered their mixed-up message. And that's why for hundreds of years, Samoan men were tattooed and women were not.

PE'A AND MALU

In Samoa today, both men and women have tattoos, but often in different styles. Men's tattoos (*pe'a*) usually cover more of the body than women's tattoos (*malu*).

HUMAN MIGRATION

There must have been more adventurous sisters like Tilafaiga and Taema in ancient history because at first humans only lived in Africa. But some traveled vast distances, even over oceans, until humans lived on every continent.

INANNA & ERESHKIGAL

THIS ANCIENT MESOPOTAMIAN MYTH HELPED PEOPLE ACCEPT THAT LIFE'S NOT FAIR

Some historians think that life was fairer for people who lived in the Stone Age. But then humans invented civilization, and life started to become more unfair. Civilization means people building cities and having jobs, instead of roaming across the Earth happy and free, hunting wild animals and living under the stars. Mesopotamia, an area in the Middle East, was the first civilization. People in Mesopotamia told a story of two sisters that didn't have a happy ending. It shows us that even 5,000 years ago, humans were figuring out that life wasn't fair.

Inanna, goddess of the Great Above, was selfish and mean, but she kept getting away with it. Her sister Ereshkigal, goddess of the Great Below, thought that was very unfair. Then one day, Inanna picked a fight she couldn't win, and Ereshkigal's husband had to join the battle to save Inanna. He saved her, but he died doing it. Ereshkigal was so angry! She was about to have a baby, whose father was now dead. So when Inanna visited the Great Below, Ereshkigal turned her sister into a piece of rotting meat and hung it on the wall.

Soon it was time for the baby to be born. Ereshkigal was hurting and afraid—until two demons came to help her. When Ereshkigal asked, "How can I ever thank you?" the demons replied, "We ask only for the rotting meat hanging on the wall." They had come to help Inanna escape! They took the meat and brought Inanna back to life, and she lived selfishly ever after.

CUNEIFORM

Old stories like this one were written by pushing a pointy stick into wet clay. This type of writing is called cuneiform. Symbols represent sounds, like most alphabets today.

XTABAY & UTZ COLEL

SOME SAY TWO ANCIENT SISTERS—ONE KIND AND ONE CRUEL—ARE STILL HAUNTING THE MAYAN JUNGLE

MALE DOMINANCE

How come in history, men often had all the power? This is called patriarchy. It's possible humans haven't always been this way—historians are still trying to find that out. But Xtabay's story reminds us that all across the world, men usually had much more power than women.

THE UNDERWORLD

In the Yucatán, there are thousands of watery underground caves. Some Maya believe they are the realm of the dead!

Long ago, legend says that a woman named Xtabay lived in a village in the Mexican rainforest. She was kind and beautiful. She always helped her neighbors. But she didn't like obeying rules. Her sister, Utz Colel, always followed the rules, but she was coldhearted and selfish. Which of the sisters do you think is the villain?

Everyone liked Xtabay, because even though she was disobedient, she was kind to everyone, even animals. Utz Colel was so jealous, she spread a rumor that her sister was actually wicked.

That night, a group of men attacked Xtabay and left her dead at the roots of a giant ceiba tree. When the villagers found her body the next morning, hundreds of beautiful-smelling flowers had grown around her overnight. Utz Colel was horrified and tore up the flowers, but they grew right back.

Utz Colel soon died mysteriously. And when the villagers found her, her body was surrounded by hundreds of stinky cactus flowers.

Today among the Maya people of the Yucatán Peninsula, old folks still tell their grandchildren this story. They warn that if you go out late at night, you might see the ghostly long-haired Xtabay, lingering among the roots of a ceiba tree. (In some versions of the story, Utz Colel is there too.) Xtabay waits, they say, to lure men down to the Underworld. They disappear forever, through the deep roots of the ceiba tree. Maybe she's trying to make sure no woman is ever attacked again.

DRUSILLA, AGRIPPINA & JULIA

IN ANCIENT ROME, THREE SISTERS CHANGED THE COURSE OF THE EMPIRE. BUT AT WHAT COST?

A FITTING TRIBUTE

Roman coins always showed the emperor's face. But Caligula insisted that his three sisters be included too! Women had never appeared on Roman coins before.

When their father was murdered, Drusilla, Agrippina, Julia, and their three older brothers knew who to blame: Tiberius, the emperor! Could the six children avenge their father's death without getting killed themselves? They decided to try.

First, they knew they needed to get the Roman people to love them—and hate the emperor. So they staged a tragic scene in which all six children carried the ashes of their father to Rome, the capital city of the empire. Heartbroken crowds said, "What an outrage that these sweet children's father was killed!" The people were on their side.

Next, the sisters befriended the emperor. They pretended to be grateful to him for sparing their lives. But secretly, they shared what they learned about him with spies, who wanted to drive him mad. Sure enough, the emperor started feeling angry and confused. He didn't know who to trust anymore. The sisters told him only they were loyal to him, and that their brother Caligula should be the next emperor. It worked!

NEW EMPEROR

Agrippina started as the sister of an emperor, then went on to be the wife of another and the mother of a third—Emperor Nero.

When Caligula became emperor, everyone knew who really had all the power: his three sisters. Everyone had to swear an oath of loyalty to "the emperor and his sisters." But when Drusilla died suddenly, Caligula blamed Agrippina and Julia. He banished them to desert islands off the coast of Italy. While they were gone, Caligula was assassinated. The sisters returned to Rome, where they would be powerful leaders for years to come.

THE EMPIRE

Rome started small, but it eventually ruled everything from North Africa to Britain and Iraq to Portugal. So Romans were a mix of different races, cultures, and religions. As long as you obeyed the law, it didn't matter where you came from!

LIFE IN ANCIENT ROME

For 1,000 years, Rome dominated Europe. For the first 500 years it was a republic, run by the people. For the second 500 years it was an empire, under the control of a powerful emperor. (Drusilla, Agrippina, and Julia helped make that change happen.) Big things like governments and borders changed, but everyday Roman life mostly stayed the same.

GARUM

Everyone's favorite treat was a sauce called *garum*. To make it, fill a barrel with fish guts. Add salt. Seal the barrel and leave it to rot for six months. When you open it again, you'll have smelly brown sludge. Delicious!

SLAVE LABOR

One of the grisly truths about Rome is that it was built by slaves. Slaves were usually people who were captured by pirates or in battle. They had a cruel life: They could often be identified by the bruises all over their body.

PETS

Romans loved keeping dogs as pets, but not cats! Some people even had their front step tiled with a picture of their dog. Underneath they wrote, "*CAVE CANEM*"—"BEWARE OF DOG."

PUBLIC TOILETS

Using the toilet was a group activity in ancient Rome. Bathrooms could have 40 toilet seats along a bench, and you would sit and chat with your friends! Underneath, a trough of running water washed away anything stinky. Can you imagine?

ARENAS

Sports were as popular back then as they are today. But in Rome, matches were often *to the death*! Huge crowds cheered and booed in giant stone arenas as gladiators fought wild animals—and each other. Gladiators were sports superstars, but they were also slaves who were forced to fight.

CLEOPATRA & ARSINOË

ONE OF HISTORY'S MOST DRAMATIC SIBLING RIVALRIES CHANGED THE FATE OF EGYPT FOREVER

Before the Egyptian pharaoh Ptolemy the 12th died, he divided his kingdom up among his children. He decided his oldest daughter, Cleopatra, and son, Ptolemy the 13th, should rule Egypt. His daughter Arsinoë and son Ptolemy the 14th, meanwhile, got to rule the Mediterranean island of Cyprus. (You might have noticed that pharaohs weren't too creative when it came to naming their kids.)

At first, everyone accepted this. But Cleopatra soon got tired of sharing the throne with her brother—he was only ten years old! So she kicked him out. But Ptolemy the 13th didn't go quietly, and soon his army was battling Cleopatra's in the Egyptian city of Alexandria. Meanwhile, Arsinoë wasn't too happy about getting stuck with Cyprus, or with Ptolemy the 14th (he was only eight!), while Cleopatra got all of Egypt. So soon Arsinoë was fighting too.

When the powerful Roman emperor Julius Caesar took Cleopatra's side, Arsinoë and Ptolemy the 13th decided to join forces. By attacking together, they hoped to defeat their sister. And it worked, at least for a while. Arsinoë and Ptolemy the 13th's army kept Cleopatra trapped in her own palace for months. But they didn't understand who they were up against. Cleopatra was clever, crafty, and popular with other rulers like Caesar—and with her people. When Caesar's army arrived to fight for Cleopatra, the younger siblings were doomed. At the brutal Battle of the Nile, Cleopatra's armies were finally victorious. She ruled Egypt until her death in 30 BCE.

TEMPLE OF ARTEMIS

After her defeat, Arsinoë was exiled to the Temple of Artemis in Ionia (modern-day Turkey). But five years later, Cleopatra had her strangled to death on the temple steps.

DEATH BY SNAKE?

Some experts say Cleopatra died after letting a venomous snake bite her. But others think it's more likely she drank poison or was murdered.

Pharaohs, the rulers of Egypt, were buried inside these marvels of engineering. Then the entrance was hidden, to prevent grave robbers from stealing the riches inside. It didn't work: Every pyramid was looted long ago. However, new scans have revealed two giant chambers in the center of the Great Pyramid of Giza—what could be inside?

ANCIENT EGYPT

It's surprising, but true: Cleopatra and Arsinoë are closer to *us* in time than they were to the builders of the pyramids! Egypt dominated the ancient world for thousands of years. You can think of ancient Egypt as having three main time periods: First, they built pyramids. Second, they stopped building pyramids and started mummifying everybody. Third, they spent centuries conquering their neighbors. But when a mysterious "Sea People" invaded around 1200 BCE, ancient Egypt collapsed. We still don't know who the Sea People were! Hundreds of years later Cleopatra and Arsinoë's family arrived on the scene.

PTOLEMAIC EMPIRE

Long after ancient Egypt collapsed, the Ptolemies—Cleopatra and Arsinoë's ancestors—put Egypt back together. Women weren't allowed to rule, so the sisters ruled through their brothers. But Cleopatra made friends with a couple of fierce Roman generals, Julius Caesar and Marc Antony. She only had to ask and they would do whatever she wanted, including kill her siblings.

PTOLEMY 12

PTOLEMY 13

JULIUS CAESAR

MARC ANTONY

THE BATTLE OF ACTIUM

Julius Caesar brought Cleopatra to Rome, but people hated her. Then Caesar was murdered! So Cleopatra escaped with Marc Antony and raised an army to fight Rome. An epic sea battle ended it all: The Egyptian fleet got stuck in the water, unable to move. We still don't know why.

TRUNG TRAC & TRUNG NHI

THOUGH THEIR COURAGEOUS REBELLION WAS CRUSHED 2,000 YEARS AGO, THESE WARRIOR SISTERS ARE STILL BELOVED SYMBOLS OF VIETNAM

Once upon a time, a Lac—a mystical red bird with a long beak—appeared to ancient tribes in southern China. With outstretched wings it led the people on a dangerous journey to a new home: Vietnam.

That was the story Trung Trac and Trung Nhi heard as children from their tribe, the Lac people, in the year 20 CE. The Lac were happy, until a new governor arrived who was violent and cruel. He never guessed that young Trac and Nhi were training in combat, dreaming of the day they would drive him out.

Finally, they were ready. Legend says, "with her raised arm and one single yell," Trung Trac rallied the people. Rebels from 65 towns joined the sisters' army and the Trung sisters led the charge, riding on top of war elephants. The governor ran away—and Trung Trac became queen!

When the far-away emperor learned of the rebellion, he sent his most fearsome general with an army 32,000 strong. Once again the sisters mounted their elephants to defend their home. They fought bravely and ferociously, but it was a lost cause. All the rebels were killed, and the general took the sisters' famous bronze war drums and melted them down. He sent the bronze to the emperor—along with the heads of Trung Trac and Trung Nhi.

HOW DID THEY DIE?

Some say the sisters didn't die—they ran away. Others say they hurled themselves into a river rather than be captured by the general. Another version says when the time came, the sisters floated off into the heavens.

"TO SLAY THE PEOPLE'S FOE AND WREAK REVENGE, TWO SISTERS TOOK UP ARMS FOR THEIR JUST CAUSE..."

FROM THE 15TH CENTURY POEM "HOMAGE TO THE QUEENS"

AGE OF EMPIRES

The Trung sisters were alive during what is called human history's "second wave." This was a period when three empires dominated the world for 1,000 years: Rome in Europe, the Parthian Empire in the Near East, and China in the Far East. While lots of other nations rose and fell, these three were the biggest.

ROMAN EMPIRE

PARTHIAN EMPIRE

HAN DYNASTY CHINA

A LASTING LEGACY

Many of history's greatest heroes failed. The Trung sisters, like so many others, decided to risk it all for their goal, and lost. But centuries later, it's clear that winning and losing doesn't matter so much as living a brave, passionate life. Even though they didn't permanently change the world in their lifetimes, their stories were told and retold. The Trung sisters became icons of what it is to be Vietnamese.

VIETNAM WAR

In the 1960s, Vietnam was once again at war. In the city of Saigon, a giant statue of Trac and Nhi inspired thousands of women to join the army. Unlike most countries, Vietnam encouraged women to fight—maybe because Vietnamese women have always been warriors! Today, a new monument in Hanoi made from war wreckage features a picture of a female soldier.

HAI BÀ TRUNG

Every February, the people of Vietnam celebrate the Trung sisters with a special holiday. Young girls dress up like the sisters, and towns host pageants and feasts. The biggest celebration is at Hai Bà Trung Temple in Hanoi, built to honor their memory.

"THEIR SHRINE SHALL STAND, A MONUMENT TO PEERLESS WOMANHOOD."

"HOMAGE TO THE TRUNG QUEENS"

FATIMA & MARIUM
AL-FIHRI

WHEN THEIR COMMUNITY WAS TURNED UPSIDE DOWN, THESE SISTERS GAVE THEIR NEIGHBORS THE PRICELESS GIFT OF EDUCATION

When Fatima and Marium al-Fihri were children, their family was forced out of their home in Tunisia, in North Africa, and moved to Morocco. Other Muslim families were being kicked out of nearby countries too. They were all grateful to find a safe home in a city called Fez. But with so many immigrants from different countries pouring into Morocco, there weren't enough teachers for everyone who wanted to learn! So when their father died and left them his money, the sisters decided to help.

They used the money to build two new mosques—places for Muslims to worship—in the city. In these beautiful buildings, people could gather to pray and build new communities together. And in each mosque's madrassa—its school—students could study religion, astronomy, architecture, mathematics, music, and more. Fatima's mosque was called the Al-Qarawiyyin and Marium's was the Mosque of the Andalusians. The sisters helped design the buildings and oversaw the construction themselves. But even though both mosques were created by women, schools had a "no girls allowed" policy in 10th century Morocco. Girls had to learn at home from their parents or private teachers, if they got to study at all.

Finishing the mosques took 18 years—but it was worth it! And more than 1,000 years after they were completed, the sisters' gift is still changing lives. Now teaching both women and men, Fatima's madrassa was renamed the University of Al-Qarawiyyin in 1963. It's recognized as the oldest university in the world.

MODERN MADRASSAS

Today, both girls and boys might attend a madrassa, though classes are usually separate. Instead of handwritten parchment books, like they had in the days of Fatima and Marium, students might now use laptops. They can study engineering, coding, or chemistry alongside their religious studies. But the students' passion for learning remains the same!

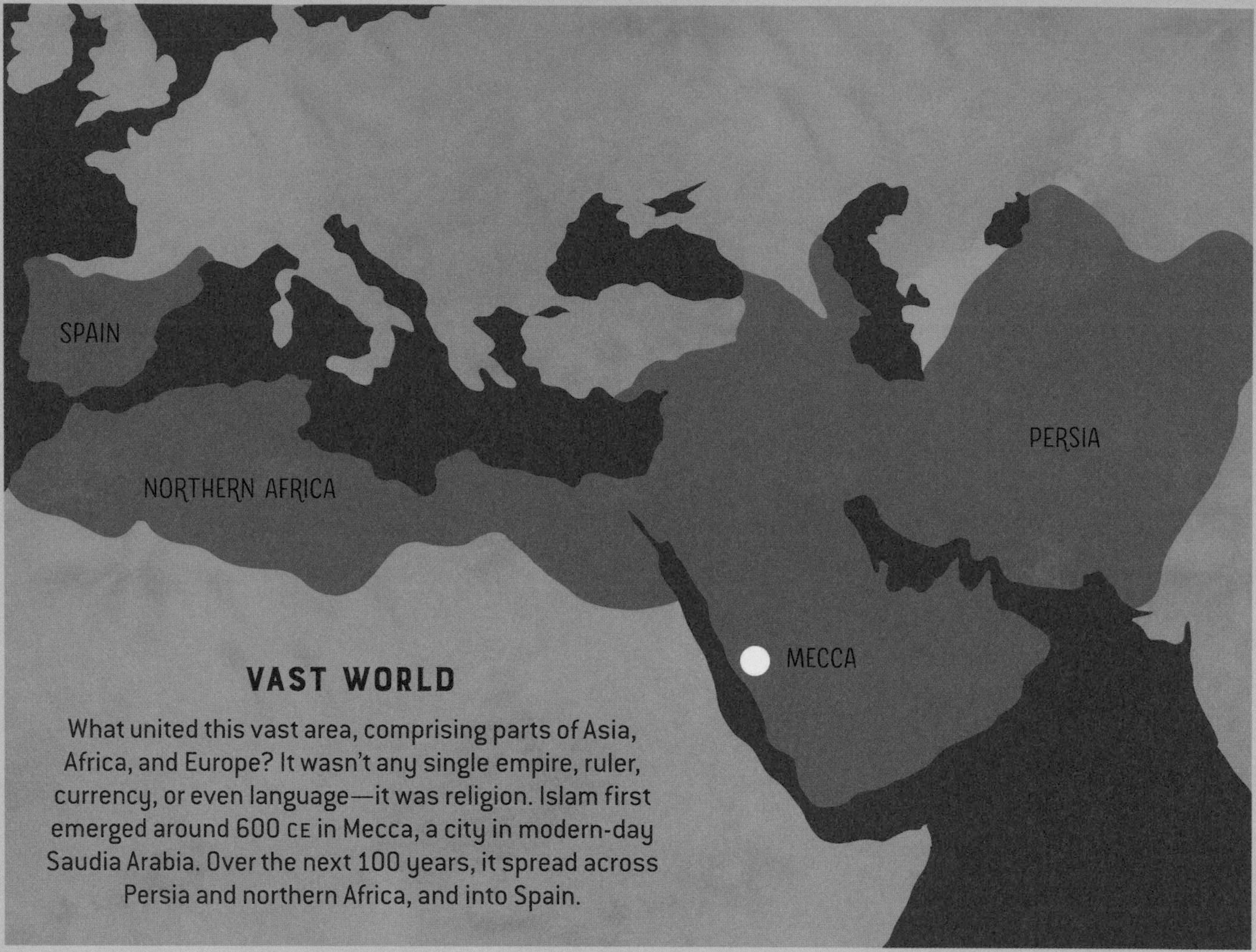

SPAIN

NORTHERN AFRICA

PERSIA

○ MECCA

VAST WORLD

What united this vast area, comprising parts of Asia, Africa, and Europe? It wasn't any single empire, ruler, currency, or even language—it was religion. Islam first emerged around 600 CE in Mecca, a city in modern-day Saudia Arabia. Over the next 100 years, it spread across Persia and northern Africa, and into Spain.

THE ISLAMIC WORLD
IN THE MIDDLE AGES

The Islamic world that Fatima and Marium lived in was the center of human learning for 1,000 years. Few places in Europe, Africa, or Asia were peaceful enough for scholars to thrive. So intelligent people from all over the world gathered in grand cities like Cordoba, Baghdad, and Cairo with the aim of improving human knowledge together! The key thing they all agreed on was that they were there to *learn from*, not *preach to*, one another.

ONE THOUSAND AND ONE NIGHTS

What was life like in the Islamic World? Our best source is a collection of 1,001 folktales. It weaves tales of magic lamps and pirates with stories about legal debates and farming methods. Altogether, it's a great snapshot of everyday life!

SCHEHERAZADE AND SHAHRYAR FROM ONE THOUSAND AND ONE NIGHTS

THE BIRTH OF UNIVERSITIES

Before the invention of colleges and universities, if you wanted to learn something, you had to find someone with that knowledge, follow them around, and beg them to teach you! Now our teachers come to us, and there are 25,000 colleges and universities across the world. The al-Fihris really started something!

EGGPLANTS AND ARTICHOKES

AVICENNA ADVANCED OUR UNDERSTANDING OF MEDICINE

THE REBEC, A STRINGED INSTRUMENT

INCREDIBLE INVENTIONS

The Islamic world was responsible for many inventions we still use today. Clever people discovered how to farm artichokes and eggplants. They gave the world new musical instruments and medicines. They figured out a drawing hack to make things look 3D. And they brought numbers from India to Europe. Imagine trying to do math with Roman numerals!

THE **SONG** SISTERS

IN A KINGDOM WHERE GIRLS WERE KEPT IN THE BACKGROUND, THE SONG SISTERS BROKE ALL THE RULES

In Tang Dynasty China (618 to 906 CE) girls weren't meant to write poetry. They weren't really even meant to learn to read! So the father of the Song sisters was supposed to raise them to be quiet and obedient. But instead, he taught Ruoshen, Ruozhao, Ruoxian, Ruolun, and Ruoxun to be scholars, poets, and philosophers. The sisters were smart, dedicated students, and they quickly became famous for their beautiful poetry.

Now, Emperor Dezong *loved* poetry. He loved it so much, he spent hours every day reading it and talking about it. The emperor wondered if the Songs really were as talented as everyone said, so he invited all five sisters to the palace. They took turns answering the trickiest questions the emperor could think up and never made a single mistake! Emperor Dezong was so pleased, he made the Song sisters official court scholars. They were the only female court scholars in the kingdom.

The sisters moved to the palace, happily advising the emperor, tutoring his children, and writing poetry for the rest of their lives. Emperor Dezong came to trust Song Ruozhao so much, he put her in charge of running the entire palace. The five Song sisters were so talented and wise, they are still remembered more than 1,000 years later.

TEACHING THE EMPERORS

Song Ruozhao was the only person Emperor Dezong trusted to tutor Prince Muzong, the future emperor. She would become the most important teacher for three different emperors before she died.

EDUCATION
IN THE TANG DYNASTY

Education was a big deal during the Tang Dynasty. You might spend the first 30 years of your life studying for a test! It was the most difficult test in the world, and if you passed it, you became a powerful government official. The test was meant to select only the smartest, wisest people to rule China, no matter where they came from or how rich they were. But ancient evidence shows us that people desperate to pass tried anything—even cheating!

GREAT INVENTIONS

China's culture of learning led to amazing things. The world's first clock was invented using a water wheel, which also powered the world's first air conditioner. And when a famous alchemist mixed charcoal, saltpeter, and sulfur, it exploded! He had discovered gunpowder, which could be used in fireworks.

> **"EDUCATION BREEDS CONFIDENCE. CONFIDENCE BREEDS HOPE. HOPE BREEDS PEACE."**
>
> **CONFUCIUS**

IMPERIAL EXAM

Imagine taking a test where you had to prove you'd memorized every book ever written. Questions asked things like, "What is the 14th word in the second paragraph of part six of Confucius' Analects?" The test was meant to measure whether you knew all things that could be known in the world. No pressure!

Tang scholars' robes still exist, with secret writing inside the clothes to help them cheat!

To prevent cheating, students were locked into exam cells for three days while they took the test.

Chinese scholars looked up to the ancient philosopher Confucius, who said we should honor and obey our elders.

The Confucius Temple in Beijing still has tablets inscribed with the names of everyone who passed the Imperial Exam.

THE KHATUN

WITHOUT THE DAUGHTERS OF GENGHIS KHAN, THERE WOULD HAVE BEEN NO MONGOL EMPIRE

Genghis Khan conquered all of Asia 800 years ago, creating the largest contiguous empire in history. (That means the empire was all connected; it wasn't in scattered pieces.) But ruling an empire is very different from smashing your enemies—and Genghis specialized in smashing. So he put his daughters in charge! Four very different sisters became Khatun (queens) over four very different regions. Their job was not just to rule, but to build a whole new empire from scratch. It was a big job, and they nailed it. There is no other time in history when women ruled over such a vast empire and so many people.

ALAQAI-BEKI

CHECHEYIGEN

Alaqai-Beki ruled the south. She learned to read and write, because her job was to mastermind a new government. She wanted people to feel they belonged in the Mongol Empire, so she declared that people could believe whatever they wanted. Still, her people rebelled. Her father wanted to kill them all, but she made him forgive everyone.

Checheyigen was sent to rule over the frozen north of Siberia. Her region was the most wild, but that suited her. She joined the locals in wearing furs and hunting on snow and ice.

Al-Altun was the shrewd businesswoman. She ruled the east, where merchants traded goods from all over the world, which meant she had to speak many languages. Her clothes came from around the globe, she wore a Greek crown, and she sat on a golden Chinese throne.

Temelun, who ruled over the west, was famous for beating men in wrestling contests and winning horse races. She also loved fighting, which turned out badly for her people. When they rebelled, she called up her father's army and had everyone killed!

AL-ALTUN　　　　　**TEMELUN**

THE MONGOL EMPIRE

The whole world was surprised when the Mongols, a small tribe in the highlands of northern Asia, conquered the continent! For 100 years, the Mongols seemed unstoppable. They crisscrossed Asia, conquering cities including Delhi, Baghdad, and Beijing. But once Genghis Khan was done fighting, his daughters set about building a lasting empire. That meant roads, laws, schools, and shops—all the things you need in a thriving society. Some call this time the *Pax Mongolica*, which means "the Mongolian peace." Life was peaceful, plentiful, and stable (for those who survived, at least!).

SILK

GENGHIS KHAN

Genghis Khan wasn't really his name—it was his title. His name when he was born was Temuchin, and he was the son of the Mongol warlord. But when his father was murdered, the Mongol tribe abandoned young Temuchin and his mother. His mother taught him how to fight. She told him his destiny was to lead the Mongols and conquer anyone who hurt them. She was right.

TAKING AN EMPIRE

The Mongol Empire—shown here in orange—was massive. As the empire expanded, the Mongols fought new armies with very different skills. It didn't matter; the Mongols' strategy was to learn from enemies, then beat them at their own game! They learned to fight on elephants, trek on camels, build a navy, and even besiege castles.

"IN THEIR LIFETIME THEY COULD NOT BE IGNORED, BUT WHEN THEY LEFT THE SCENE, HISTORY CLOSED THE DOOR BEHIND THEM AND LET THE DUST OF CENTURIES COVER THEIR TRACKS."

JACK WEATHERFORD ON THE KHATUN

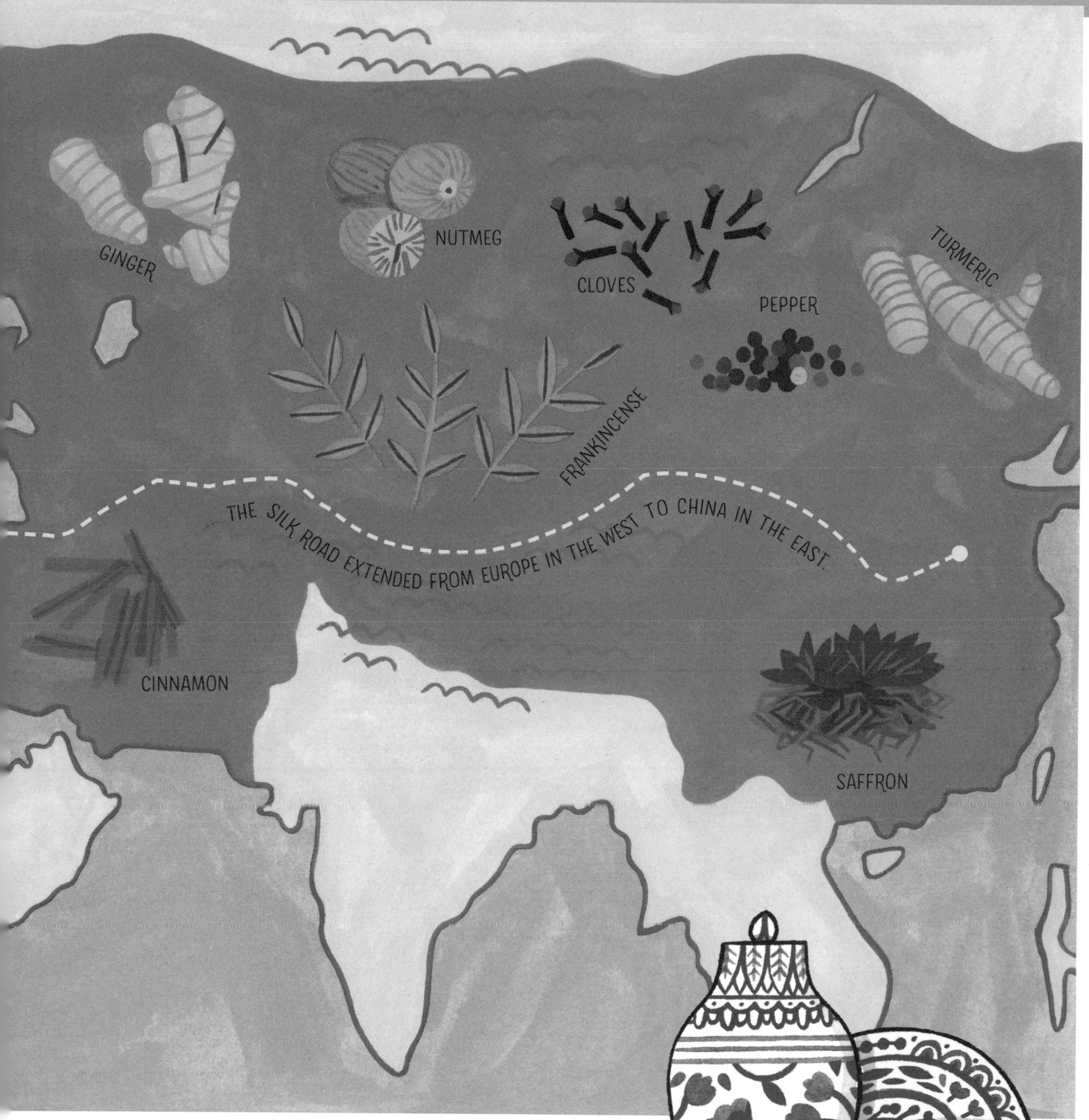

GINGER

NUTMEG

CLOVES

PEPPER

TURMERIC

FRANKINCENSE

... THE SILK ROAD EXTENDED FROM EUROPE IN THE WEST TO CHINA IN THE EAST.

CINNAMON

SAFFRON

THE SILK ROAD

The Mongols ruled the world's biggest trading network: the Silk Road. It was the first and only time the whole road was under one empire. The Khatun wanted trade to thrive, so they harshly punished thieves and robbers that had been attacking merchants for years. Goods traded along the Silk Road included porcelain, spices, and (you guessed it) silk.

PORCELAIN

LITTLE BROTHER

Edward was the youngest sibling, but because he was a boy, he inherited the throne first. He was only nine years old!

DIFFERENT MOTHERS

Mary's mother was Catherine of Aragon, a Catholic; Elizabeth's mother was Anne Boleyn, a Protestant. Both died when their daughters were young, and the girls spent their lives fighting for their mothers' beliefs.

MARY & ELIZABETH
TUDOR

WHAT MATTERS MORE: STANDING UP FOR YOUR BELIEFS OR LOVING YOUR FAMILY?

Sometimes people feel so passionate about what they believe, that they will do anything. They are willing to die, or even kill, for it! Five hundred years ago, two English princesses grew up during a horrible war within the Christian religion. Mary was on the Catholic side of the religion, while her half sister Elizabeth was on the Protestant side. The sisters kept wondering if they should be allies or enemies. How would you feel if you loved your sister but were told that her beliefs were evil?

Then their little brother, Edward, who was the king, died very young. Mary, the oldest, was next in line to the throne, followed by Elizabeth. They may have had a chance to bring the warring sides together, but it seems they chose religion over sisterhood. Mary became queen and locked her sister away in a tower! Then she joined the fight against Protestants. She even had people burned alive for what they believed. She is called Bloody Mary because of all the Protestants who died while she ruled. But she didn't kill Elizabeth.

Mary only ruled for five years before she died of cancer. Elizabeth became queen at the age of 18 and the tables were turned. She had Catholics burned alive for their beliefs. Elizabeth ordered the deaths of just as many people as her sister Mary had—maybe more!

What if these sisters had united England with their love, rather than joined in the fight? Could love have conquered hate?

ELIZABETH

MARY

TUDOR TIMES

England during the time of Mary and Elizabeth was chaotic, but the 16th century (1500s) was a time of huge change all across the globe too. To start it off, Europeans learned that there was an entire continent they didn't realize existed across the ocean: the Americas. It was full of people they hadn't ever heard about, food they hadn't ever tasted, and animals they hadn't ever seen. Can you even imagine if something like that happened today? People started wondering, *what else don't we know?!*

HENRY VIII

Henry VIII, the Tudor king, is one of the most infamous rulers in history. *Infamous* means you're famous—for being terrible! He was strong, had a bold personality, and had six wives. He once swore an oath to be the ultimate protector of the Catholic religion, but a few years later, he became its number-one enemy! No wonder his kids, Mary and Elizabeth, had such different beliefs.

SPANISH ARMADA

In 1588, Catholic Spain attacked Elizabeth I's England with a fleet of ships. Spain said it was a righteous cause, to wipe out Protestants. But a storm blew in and destroyed the Spanish fleet. English people dubbed it "The Protestant Wind."

GUTENBERG PRESS

For most of history, books were rare and cost as much as a car does today! That's because they were all handmade. But when Johannes Gutenberg invented the printing press, which could produce books quickly and cheaply, knowledge could be shared across the world more easily.

RELIGIOUS REFORMATION

It wasn't just the Christian religion that had a dramatic split in the 1500s. All over the world, other religions did the same. Buddhists, Muslims, Jews, Hindus, and Confucians all had to rethink what they believed as new ideas appeared. Maybe it was all the surprises of the 1500s, plus new books to read, that made people see the world anew.

ANNA & BRITA ZIPPEL

SWEDISH SISTERS WERE ACCUSED OF WITCHCRAFT, CAUSING A SCANDAL THAT ROCKED SOCIETY TO THE CORE

Even though they were sisters, Brita and Anna Zippel were very different. Anna was wealthy, fashionable, and popular. Brita was a poor beggar who was always picking fights and arguing with neighbors. But when the "witch mania," called "*Det Stora Oväsendet*" ("The Great Noise"), began sweeping across Sweden, some people stopped arguing with annoying neighbors... and started accusing them of witchcraft instead!

Brita was suspected of being a witch several times—maybe because of her odd behavior, possibly because a disease made her husband's nose fall off! But then one day, when respectable sister Anna was out walking, a young boy pointed right at her and shouted, "She's the witch who took me to Blåkulla!" Blåkulla was a legendary island where people said the Devil lived. Anna was astonished. She probably thought nobody would believe his story. But as the panic in Stockholm grew, more children accused both Zippel sisters and the stories they told grew wilder every day.

Some claimed that Anna was the "Queen of Blåkulla" who kidnapped young brides for the Devil, and even Brita's own daughter accused her of plotting to burn down the royal palace using her magic powers! The sisters protested their innocence, swearing they had never practiced magic, seen the Devil, or hurt children. But witch trials were almost never fair, and both sisters were convicted of witchcraft. Brita and Anna Zippel were beheaded together in the town square in front of a crowd of cheering onlookers.

THE TRIAL

The Zippels were tried inside Katarina Church in Stockholm, along with six other women. By the time the "Great Noise" witch mania ended, 280 people had been executed throughout Sweden.

THEIR ACCOMPLICE?

Anna Månsdotter was also convicted of witchcraft alongside the Zippels. People claimed the herbal medicines she made and sold, with help from her friend Anna Zippel, were actually magic potions!

SALEM WITCH TRIALS

In 1692, Elizabeth Parris (age nine) and Abigail Williams (age 11) of Salem, Massachusetts, started having "fits." When doctors blamed witchcraft, Salem began a mania like no other. More than 200 were accused, and 20 people were executed.

WITCH MANIA

People have believed in magic for most of human history. But around 1550, towns across Europe started putting people on trial for the crime of witchcraft. Everyone in town watched: It was juicy entertainment! About half the time, the person was set free, while those who refused to confess were burned alive. But how can you prove witchcraft using facts and evidence in court? After a century of trials, people realized it wasn't possible, and witch mania ended.

HOW TO SPOT A WITCH

Records from witch trials tell us what people believed was "evidence" of witchcraft 400 years ago. Common accusations at trials included claims a woman was seen flying at night, or that she gave birth to monsters or animals. People could arouse suspicion because their medicines worked very well, or maybe their neighbors' goats or cows had mysteriously died. Sometimes a woman could be accused of witchcraft simply because she had appeared in someone else's dream!

DUNKING TEST

If someone thought they'd got a witch they would try dunking her in a river or lake using a "ducking stool." They'd plunge her under the water and wait. If she came back up alive, she must have used magic to survive, so she was a witch! If she drowned, she was innocent… Oops.

QUEEN NZINGA & QUEEN MUKAMBU

ROYAL SIBLINGS WHO WORKED TOGETHER TO PROTECT THEIR COUNTRY FROM OUTSIDE FORCES

Even as a child, Nzinga was unusually smart and brave. She was also very good at fighting—especially with a battle-ax! Maybe that was why Nzinga, not her sister Mukambu, was their father's favorite. He ruled the Kingdom of Ndongo (modern-day Angola) in southern Africa. But when he died in 1617, Nzinga and Mukambu's brother Ngola Mbandi claimed the throne. To make sure nobody could challenge him, the new king had Nzinga's young son killed. Worried she would be next, Nzinga fled to a nearby kingdom for safety. But when his war with Portugal started to go badly, King Mbandi asked Nzinga for help. She agreed to come back, and she helped her brother negotiate peace with the Portuguese.

When Mbandi died three years later (some say his sister poisoned him, others think he did it himself) Nzinga took charge. Now it was her turn to kill her brother's son in order keep power for herself. Officially queen, she teamed up with her sister Mukambu to keep the Portuguese out of the kingdom. Working together—and making deals with other countries for support—the sisters made a powerful pair. So to try to force Nzinga to give up, the Portuguese kidnapped Mukambu and sailed off with her as a hostage! She was only released when Nzinga and the Portuguese finally agreed on a new peace treaty—*ten years* later. Together again, Nzinga and Mukambu continued to fight off other threats to the kingdom. And when Nzinga died at 82 years old, Mukambu took over as queen of an independent Ndongo.

POWER PLAY

While deep in negotiations, the Portuguese governor tried to make Nzinga sit on the floor, while he sat on a fancy throne. But Nzinga's servant knelt to form a human chair for her—showing she was just as important as the governor!

THE SLAVE TRADE

In Africa, like so many places across the world, taking and trading people as slaves was something people had always done. But when European countries started to sail to Africa in the 16th century, they bought slaves by the hundreds—and then thousands. European slave ships then sailed to the Americas to deliver enslaved people to giant farms called plantations. It was a horrible and cruel industry, responsible for millions of deaths over hundreds of years.

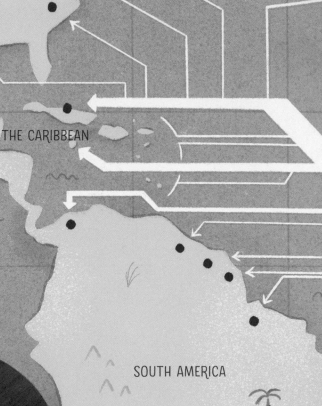

NORTH AMERICA

THE CARIBBEAN

SOUTH AMERICA

NZINGA'S KINGDOM

Humans are complicated—in the past just as they are now. Queen Nzinga created special sanctuaries (safe places to live) for people who had escaped slavery in nearby countries. But she also sold slaves to the Portuguese as part of her peace treaty with them.

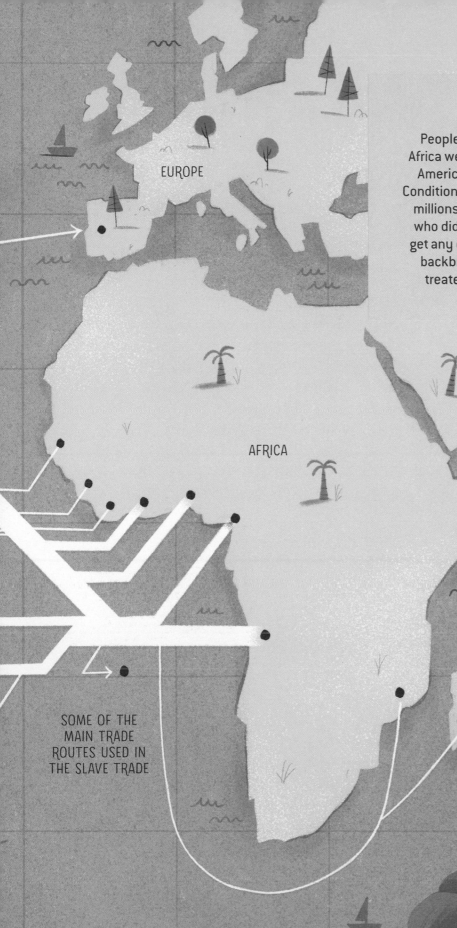

EUROPE

AFRICA

SOME OF THE
MAIN TRADE
ROUTES USED IN
THE SLAVE TRADE

SLAVE ROUTES

People who were captured and enslaved in Africa were sent by ship to plantations in North America, the Caribbean, and South America. Conditions on board the ships were dreadful, and millions didn't survive the voyages. For those who did make it to the Americas, life wouldn't get any easier. Working on the plantations was backbreaking work, and the enslaved were treated despicably by plantation owners.

COLUMBIAN EXCHANGE

In 1492, the Italian sailor Christopher Columbus landed in the Americas, setting in motion a trading of goods between Europe and the Americas. Foods not found in Europe, such as tomatoes, potatoes, and chocolate, made their way across the ocean. Humans were sent the other way as slaves.

JAHANARA &

WHEN A FAMILY GOES TO WAR AGAINST ITSELF, SISTERHOOD GETS COMPLICATED

Four hundred years ago in the city of Agra, in what is now India, Jahanara and Roshanara Begum were born in a palace of the famous Mughal Empire. The two oldest daughters of Emperor Shah Jahan and his favorite wife Mumtaz Mahal, the sisters played chess and polo together and studied religion, poetry, and painting. Both princesses were clever and brave. They probably expected to live together for the rest of their lives, helping their father and brothers rule the kingdom. But when the emperor became ill, the family started to break apart.

Shah Jahan wanted oldest brother Dara Shikoh to be the next emperor. But younger brother Aurangzeb had other plans. He put together his own army, and the brothers went to war. As the family split down the middle, the princesses had to pick a side.

AGRA FORT

The big red stone fortress where the Begum sisters grew up still stands in northern India. Tourists come from all over the world to visit it.

ROSHANARA BEGUM

Always loyal to their father, favorite daughter Jahanara chose Dara Shikoh. But younger sister Roshanara sided with Aurangzeb. As their father got sicker, the fighting got fiercer—and dirtier.

Dara Shikoh tried to lure his brother into a deadly trap, but Roshanara warned Aurangzeb just in time! Jahanara begged her brothers to divide the kingdom peacefully. They refused. Eventually, Aurangzeb won. He executed his brother and locked up his father and Jahanara in Agra Fort.

Roshanara probably expected her little brother to be grateful—she'd saved his life after all—but she was in for a nasty shock. When Emperor Shah Jahan finally died, Aurangzeb banished Roshanara from the palace and put Jahanara in charge. There would be no happy-ever-after for this princess: Aurangzeb had Roshanara secretly poisoned a few years later.

ROSHANARA'S TOMB

Roshanara was buried under a pavilion in Roshanara Garden, where she lived her last years in exile. Today, it is a park in Delhi.

TAJ MAHAL

Shah Jahan built the Taj Mahal as a tomb for Jahanara and Roshanara's mother, Mumtaz Mahal, when she died in childbirth. It's built of heavy white marble, with complicated patterns cut into the stone and filled with perfectly carved gems. The huge monument took over 20 years to finish! It's still one of the most famous buildings in the world.

THE MUGHAL EMPIRE

Roshanara and Jahanara's great-grandfather Emperor Akbar turned his small kingdom into one of the largest empires in history! With powerful armies and clever politics, he conquered most of South Asia. The Mughal Empire united millions of people with different beliefs, cultures, and languages. But though times were mostly peaceful for the people, the emperor's children were constantly fighting one another.

A GIANT EMPIRE

The Mughal Empire lasted for 300 years. It included sections of modern-day India, Pakistan, Afghanistan, Nepal, and Bangladesh. The empire was largest under Emperor Aurangzeb, but when he stopped allowing people to follow whatever religion they chose, it all began to fall apart.

LOVE STORY

Though all Mughal emperors had multiple wives, the love story between Shah Jahan and Mumtaz Mahal is so famous it's still being told today! During their marriage, Mumtaz Mahal was a powerful leader and an important voice in the court. Shah Jahan was devastated when she died.

INVENTIONS

The Mughals loved learning. Their curiosity inspired many inventions, from weapons and musical instruments to shampoo! Especially amazing are the celestial globes Shah Jahan used to study astronomy. These metal spheres are so incredible that people still can't figure out how they were made.

"MY SISTER WAS NOT OF A VERY PATIENT TEMPER, AND COULD NOT BE RECONCILED TO HAVE CHILDREN ABOUT HER.... IN SHORT, THERE WAS NO ONE WHO CARED ANYTHING ABOUT ME."

CAROLINE HERSCHEL

CAROLINE & SOPHIA
HERSCHEL

IN THIS REAL-LIFE CINDERELLA STORY, INSTEAD OF MARRYING A PRINCE, THE HEROINE BECAME AN ASTRONOMER

Caroline Herschel's childhood in Hanover, Germany, was awful. She was forced to be the servant for her large family every waking moment. She was beaten and sometimes starved, so she never grew taller than five feet. Diseases left her blind in one eye with a disfigured face and leg.

Her oldest sibling, Sophia, was beautiful and smart—everyone's favourite. Of course, she never did any work. Sophia was disgusted by Caroline's looks. She constantly shouted at Caroline to get out of her sight. Sophia married a wealthy, powerful man. It seemed she was destined for a life of success and admiration, and Caroline appeared doomed. But life is rarely what it seems.

Caroline would secretly wake in the middle of the night to read and teach herself as best she could, in case a chance for a better life ever came. And it did: Her astronomer brother, William, needed an assistant in England. Caroline was only allowed to go after William paid their mother for her.

Caroline poured her whole heart into her new life. She and William studied the stars every night. They only slept when it was cloudy. The Herschels wanted to see farther than anyone ever had, so they built the world's largest telescope in their backyard. Sure enough, through it they saw something no one else had ever seen: a *new planet*. They named it George. But astronomers around the world didn't approve and renamed it Uranus!

DANGEROUS CROSSING

To reach her brother in England, Caroline first survived a shipwreck. Locals found her and gave her new clothes. She then traveled by stagecoach, which also crashed!

SOPHIA'S FATE

Sophia did *not* live happily ever after. Her husband turned out to be a cruel man who wasted all his money, and she spent the rest of her life in misery.

THE ENLIGHTENMENT

If you love learning, the 1700s would have been an exciting time to live. Across Europe and the Americas, people began a quest for knowledge they called the Enlightenment. Their goal was to figure out the answer to life, the universe, and everything else. But no one could do it alone, so experts in different subjects formed clubs. That way, they could solve the greatest mysteries of the universe together.

ICON OF THE ENLIGHTENMENT

People loved Caroline Herschel for showing what was possible. Her life proved that we can change our destinies, and her discoveries proved that science can decode the mysteries of the universe. Whenever she went out, strangers recognized her and thanked her! How do you think her sister Sophia felt about that?

COMET HUNTING

Caroline Herschel didn't just discover planet George: She found comets and galaxies too. People called her "The Comet Huntress." They loved that she could predict the day and time a comet would appear. Awestruck crowds watched the sky light up. It felt like magic, but it was just math!

NEW KNOWLEDGE

One goal of the Enlightenment was to spread knowledge to absolutely everyone, especially those who couldn't go to school. So all the smartest people pooled their knowledge into one giant book: the world's first encyclopedia.

EXPERIMENTS

Hands-on science experiments helped spread knowledge to people who didn't want to read. (I mean, would you rather read about a chemical explosion or see one?) Scientific tools became a fashionable way to show you were part of the Enlightenment. Wealthy families even had scientific instruments made of gold to display in their houses.

OLYMPE DE GOUGES & JEANNE RAYNART

TWO SMALL-TOWN GIRLS CAME TO BE AT THE CENTER OF ONE OF THE MOST DRAMATIC REVOLUTIONS IN HISTORY

In a little French village, sisters Jeanne and Olympe were born to a butcher and a maid. When Jeanne grew up and moved to Paris, 14-year-old Olympe was left behind and forced to marry a man she hated. But her husband died soon after, and in 1770 Olympe set off to Paris to live with Jeanne.

Olympe was bright, witty, and beautiful, and Paris society soon revolved around the sisters. They were invited to all the best parties, where everyone was talking about *liberty*, which means freedom. "All men should have liberty!" they said. "It's the most important thing in the world!" Olympe became famous for saying, "How about liberty for women too?" Back then, it was a shocking idea. Olympe was even attacked in the street for saying it. Jeanne begged her to stop saying such dangerous things.

Then, in 1789, the French Revolution happened. In the name of liberty, the king was overthrown. Paris was chaotic as people fought over what to do next. Olympe couldn't stay quiet. "Women, wake up; now is the time to discover your rights!" she wrote. "It is in your power to free yourselves!" The city was covered in posters she made, and newspapers were full of things she wrote. Jeanne must have been angry—she knew how dangerous this was. Sure enough, it wasn't long before Olympe was imprisoned in a nasty, freezing cell. On November 3, 1792, she was beheaded in the main square of Paris.

GUILLOTINE

In the French Revolution thousands were executed by guillotine—a giant neck-chopping blade. Before she died, Olympe was at peace: "I know that my death is inevitable; but it is a glorious and beautiful death."

THE AGE OF REVOLUTIONS

It wasn't just France: For about 50 years, revolution spread like a fire on both sides of the Atlantic Ocean. Kings and queens were overthrown as more and more people believed they could rule themselves. None of it happened easily. Thousands of people died in horrible, brutal wars. But it would all be worth it, the rebels said: The freedom to rule ourselves would make the world a better place!

CULT OF LIBERTY

All these revolutions were born from the big ideas of the Enlightenment. Scientists, artists, and philosophers had spent a century trying to find the one, big answer to human life. And they thought they'd found it. Liberty, they said—liberty is the solution to everything! People loved the idea so much, we call their movement the "Cult of Liberty."

AMERICAN REVOLUTION

North American colonies started the age of revolutions when they rebelled against their British rulers in 1776. Rebels called themselves the "Sons of Liberty," to show they had a righteous cause. The outcome was the founding of the United States of America.

GREECE

A fierce sea captain named Bouboulina started the revolution in Greece in 1821. After years of secret planning, she defeated the ruling Ottoman Empire with a fleet of ships and her own personal army. She always fought alongside her men, on land and at sea.

HAITI

France had conquered the island of Haiti in the Caribbean and turned it into sugar plantations. In 1791, and after years of horrible treatment, the slaves in Haiti realized that liberty should apply to them too. Under the command of Toussaint Louverture they led the most successful slave revolt in history.

BRAZIL

Rebels shouted "Long live liberty!" to begin the revolution in Brazil in 1822. Anita Garibaldi joined the fight, even though she was nine months pregnant! When the revolution collapsed, Anita sailed to Italy to fight for liberty there. She won and became "the Mother of Italy."

THE BRONTË SISTERS

USING THEIR IMAGINATIONS TO CREATE NEW WORLDS, THREE SISTERS TURNED TRAGEDY INTO SOMETHING BEAUTIFUL

MASTERPIECES

Writing under the names Currer, Ellis, and Acton Bell, the Brontë sisters wrote six novels and a book of poetry. Some of their books—such as Charlotte's *Jane Eyre* and Emily's *Wuthering Heights*—are some of the most famous novels in the English language.

HOME

Haworth Parsonage is now a museum, but it was the Brontës' home for 40 years. It overlooks the cemetery where most of the family are buried.

Charlotte, Emily, and Anne Brontë were born in a time when life was hard for everyone, but they had more than their fair share of troubles. Their mother died when Anne was still a baby. Their two oldest sisters, Maria and Elizabeth, died of tuberculosis (a lung disease) four years later. So Charlotte, Emily, and Anne lived with their father, brother, and aunt in Yorkshire, England.

The Brontë children spent most of their time together. They read every book and magazine in the house, and when they ran out of stories, they made up their own. The siblings created imaginary worlds, writing wonderful stories about their make-believe kingdoms of "Angria," "Glass Town," and "Gondal." And when they grew up, those stories turned out to have been the perfect practice for becoming "real" writers!

In 1847, each sister published her first novel. But to avoid trouble and protect their privacy, the Brontës hid their identities behind fake names. The books were a hit, and the three mysterious "Bell brothers" were suddenly famous. Sadly, the youngest Brontës wouldn't enjoy their fame for long—Emily died exactly one year later, and Anne six months after that. Both died of tuberculosis, the same disease that had killed their sisters 20 years earlier. When Charlotte died in 1855, the Brontë sisters were gone—but they had left behind incredible stories.

"READING IS MY FAVORITE OCCUPATION, WHEN I HAVE LEISURE FOR IT AND BOOKS TO READ."

ANNE BRONTË

WRITING PIONEERS

Can words change the world? Throughout human history and all around the world, women, like the Brontë sisters, have been writers. From the first written words on clay tablets to e-books you can download on your phone, women have told stories, explored new ideas, and used their words to change their communities and inspire others.

MARGARET CAVENDISH

A 17th-century English writer, Margaret saw the world differently than most people. Her novel *The Blazing World*, about another planet that could be reached only from the Earth's North Pole, was the first work of science fiction ever written in English!

SOR JUANA INÉS DE LA CRUZ

Juana wanted to write poetry and music, so instead of getting married, she became a nun. She spent her life in 17th-century Mexico studying philosophy and religion, helping poor women, and writing. She wrote hundreds of books and poems fighting for women's rights.

PHILLIS WHEATLEY

At the age of seven, Phillis was kidnapped and sold into slavery. She loved to read and began writing wonderful poetry when she was a teenager. In 1772, she became the first African American woman to publish a book of poetry.

MOHLAROYIM

One of Uzbekistan's best poets, Mohlaroyim wrote in three languages— Uzbek, Tajik, and Persian—under the pen name *Nodira*. She was also an important ruler, leading the Uzbek state of Kokand after her husband died in 1822.

SWARNAKUMARI DEVI

The first Bengali woman to publish a novel, Swarnakumari also wrote plays, poems, songs, and essays in both Bengali and English. She lived in India in the 19th century.

NA HYE-SOK

Na was a courageous writer and extraordinary painter in the early 20th century. She was rejected by society for writing that women should be allowed to make art—and their own decisions! But now she's recognized as one of South Korea's greatest artists.

AGATHA CHRISTIE

English writer Agatha died in 1976, but she may still be the best-selling writer in history! Her mystery novels have sold billions of copies all over the world and been translated into more than 100 languages.

MARJANE SATRAPI

Growing up during a revolution in the 1970s, Marjane watched Iran change completely almost overnight. When the government threatened her family, her parents sent her to Europe. There she wrote her first graphic novel, *Persepolis*, about her experiences.

NAKANO TAKEKO & NAKANO YŪKO

LEADING AN ARMY OF SAMURAI WOMEN, THESE SISTERS DEFENDED TRADITION IN AN EPIC LAST STAND

Samurai warriors had controlled Japan for 800 years before Takeko and Yūko were born. Their samurai parents began teaching them to fight as soon as they could hold a sword. The sisters trained every day, and by their teens they were teaching other girls to fight.

In the 19th century, European countries and the United States were invading countries all over the world. The Japanese emperor saw that any country who resisted was destroyed. So he tried the opposite: He said, "Come teach us how to be like you!" He was hoping to stop the invaders from taking over.

Many samurai warned that this would destroy everything that made Japan unique. But with his new teachers from Europe, the emperor built a new army. His soldiers now fought with guns and cannons. But the Nakano sisters' clan resisted, and at Aizu Castle they planned a rebellion.

The emperor's army arrived on a rainy October day in 1868 to force the samurai out. They expected a fight, but they didn't expect an army of samurai women to burst from the castle! The Nakano sisters led the charge. When the soldiers saw the rebels were all women, they hesitated—giving the samurai a chance to attack. Takeko killed six soldiers before she was shot in the chest. When Yūko ran to her side, Takeko asked her to cut off her head so the enemy couldn't take it as a prize—so she did. The samurai lost the battle, and the emperor's tactics probably saved Japan, but the Nakano sisters are still celebrated as icons of courage and tradition.

NAGINATA

All female samurai fought with a "mowing-down sword," or *naginata*. It turned out to be no match for bullets, but Nakano Takeko's weapon is still on display in Aizu!

BURIAL

Nakano Yūko buried her sister's head at the foot of a pine tree at the nearby Hōkai-Ji Temple. Fifty years later, a stone monument was placed to mark her resting place.

SAMURAI WAY OF LIFE

Samurai swore to live by a code called Bushido. True samurai, they said, would never fear death, always be loyal, master strength and skill, perfect poetry or some other art, and live a humble, simple life. It was a way of life at odds with industrialization.

COLONIALISM

Industrial countries learned that they could easily take over countries that didn't have the new technology. European nations started claiming territories, or "colonies," all over the world. They said, "we're here to help you get new technology too!" But in reality they were using the colonies for their own benefit.

THE INDUSTRIAL WORLD

The Industrial Revolution might be the biggest event in the history of the world. It wasn't a war, but a revolution in technology. It started in Britain, then spread to Europe and the United States, and gave those countries technology that was so much more advanced than the rest of the world. Everything changed: The industrial countries were unstoppable.

STEAM
ENGINE

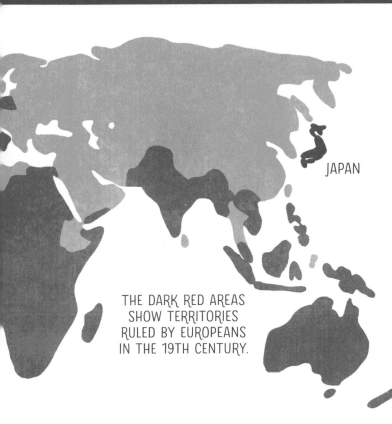

JAPAN

THE DARK RED AREAS
SHOW TERRITORIES
RULED BY EUROPEANS
IN THE 19TH CENTURY.

STEAM POWER

Steam power started the industrial revolution. For the first time in human history, people harnessed a force stronger than human or animal muscles. Steam engines pushed pistons back and forth in a cylinder—and trains and factories were born.

GATLING GUN

Just turning a crank would fire an endless stream of bullets from this new gun. People said it would save lives, because one soldier could do the work of 100. Instead, it did the opposite.

STEAMSHIPS

No longer limited by tides and wind, steam-powered ships could travel anywhere! In the United States, riverboats could now sail up rivers like the mighty Mississippi. In Japan, American steamships belching black smoke were the first to appear offshore, demanding that Japan allow the invaders in.

PAULINA & CLOTILDE
LUISI

THE LUISI SISTERS BELIEVED GIRLS COULD DO BIG THINGS—AND THEY PROVED IT

In the 1800s, most people in the South American country of Uruguay didn't think women could do anything important. But Paulina and Clotilde Luisi wanted to change the world. Their mother encouraged them to dream big, even when others laughed. Their father taught them to always help people. So even when society told them they couldn't do it, the Luisi girls kept trying.

Paulina noticed many women struggled to keep themselves and their kids healthy, so she decided to go to medical school. Clotilde believed all kids deserved a good education, so she went to law school to fight for children's rights.

After years of hard work, Paulina and Clotilde made history. Paulina became the first woman doctor in Uruguay. Clotilde became the country's first female laywer. But that was just the beginning. The sisters got to work using their skills to improve life for people all over the world. Paulina worked with the League of Nations (an organization that helps countries cooperate) to fight slavery worldwide. She taught schools smarter ways to keep students healthy and fought for women's right to vote and get an education. Clotilde knew that schools weren't treating kids with disabilities well. So she found better ways to teach deaf and blind children—then taught the country's teachers how to teach that way, too! She helped change the laws so all students in Uruguay were treated fairly. By following their big dreams, the Luisi sisters really did change the world.

Women from many different countries and cultures fought for women's suffrage—the right to vote. Some women had to wait decades longer than others to have their rights recognized, even in the same country, because of factors like the color of their skin. Some women are still waiting!

VOTES FOR WOMEN

VOTES FOR WOMEN

BREAKING DOWN BARRIERS

The late 1800s were full of important changes for women. After centuries of being bossed around by men and even sometimes treated like property, women began demanding a place in all the places they hadn't been allowed: government, science, and the arts. Some women, such as the Luisi sisters, began demanding that men treat them like equals. Standing up for women's independence, legal rights, and education, these courageous women helped change the world for women and girls everywhere.

WOMEN IN UNIVERSITIES

Women all over the world wanted an advanced education, but it took some universities a long time to accept them. Oxford, in the United Kingdom, allowed women to attend classes in 1878 but wouldn't let them earn degrees until 1920! This map shows when a few different countries allowed women to receive an advanced education.

SWEDEN 1861

RUSSIA 1764

GREECE 1890

JAPAN 1900

CUBA 1901

INDIA 1875

SOUTH AFRICA 1886

"I KNOW NOTHING OF MAN'S RIGHTS, OR WOMAN'S RIGHTS; HUMAN RIGHTS ARE ALL THAT I RECOGNIZE."

SARAH MOORE GRIMKÉ, WOMEN'S RIGHTS ACTIVIST

NATIVE AMERICANS

When Native American women were excluded from voting, education, and other new rights granted to white American women, powerful Native activists fought for change. Zitkála-Šá published important reports about the ways the United States was harming Native people. Susan La Flesche became the country's first Native American medical doctor.

PIONEERS

In 1886, three amazing women graduated from medical school in Pennsylvania. Kei Okami from Japan, Sabat Islambooly from Syria, and Anandibai Joshee from India each became their country's very first woman to earn a medical degree.

THEATRE DEBUT

In 1867, at age ten and 12, the sisters performed for the first time, in San Francisco, California. The press went wild, saying they were destined for greatness.

NEW ERA

With Sam Lucas, the sisters staged America's first play by an all-Black cast. Sam played the romantic hero, which Black men had never been allowed to do.

ANNA & EMMA HYERS

TWO SINGING SISTERS ROSE TO GREATNESS IN TROUBLED TIMES

Anna and Emma Hyers were opposites. Anna was tall and thin with a soaring high soprano voice, while Emma was strong and stocky with a voice so rich and low that she could sing male parts. They made a perfect combination. The young sisters started singing concerts together, their drastically different voices melding in perfect harmony. Their father took them on the road, and their regal voices quickly made them famous.

But the sisters wanted to do more than sing, because as they traveled across America, Anna and Emma saw that the promise of equality wasn't coming true for people of color. Racist attitudes and laws were everywhere. If they couldn't change the laws, at least they could try to change people's minds. Anna and Emma understood that the most powerful force on Earth is a good story. And they had already witnessed the power of music to make their audiences feel. So they decided to stage musicals: stories, wrapped in music, that could reach right into the hearts of audience members and help them change.

Every musical they performed featured Black heroes who gained their freedom and built strong, noble, meaningful lives. Through soaring anthems, heart-wrenching drama, and lots of hilarious comedy too, their message was clear: African Americans have infinite potential. Audiences couldn't get enough. These sisters were daring—and not just because they were staging plays that no one else dared perform. They also had their eye on Boston, Massachusetts, music capital of the United States. Concert halls rarely accepted Black musicians, and Boston's music scene was famously snobby. But the Hyers sisters went there anyway; they stepped into America's spotlight. And Boston cheered in a standing ovation!

"I WENT A MILE AND A HALF IN THE MOST FURIOUS TEMPEST OF WIND AND SNOW... TO... HEAR THEIR EXQUISITE MUSIC."

MARK TWAIN

OPERA HOUSES

Before radio, TV, or movies, the theater was the place where people could hear great musicians or see a show. People would dress up, like they were going to a fancy ball, just to sit in the audience! The rich could afford to watch from their own private balconies, called box seats.

THE POWER OF THE STAGE

In ancient history, people believed storytellers were the most powerful people of all! Called bards, they sang their stories—just like the Hyers sisters. But over the centuries, props, costumes, and eventually theaters were added. Stories came to life in incredible new ways! Today, stories are told in movies, on TV, and online. But the stage still has a special magic.

MILLIE AND CHRISTINE McKOY

Born into slavery, twins Millie and Christine were joined at the spine. As children they were kidnapped and displayed as "freaks." But after they gained their freedom, they learned to dance, sing, play piano, and speak five languages! They performed worldwide as "the Two-Headed Nightingale," then bought the farm where they'd been enslaved and lived happily ever after!

WORLD PEACE FAIR

The Hyers sisters sang at the world's first mass music festival in Boston in 1872. Great musicians performed for weeks to celebrate world peace. A giant theater could seat 100,000 people, but, as microphones and speakers hadn't been invented yet, the audience could hardly hear a thing!

BLACK MUSICAL THEATRE

The Hyers sisters would have been thrilled to see that theater today is still going strong. In Broadway hits such as *Hamilton*, Black performers tell stories of freedom through song—exactly like Anna and Emma long ago!

THE FOX SISTERS

TWO YOUNG SISTERS PRETENDED THEY COULD TALK TO THE DEAD. WHEN MILLIONS OF GROWN-UPS BELIEVED THEM, SPIRITUALISM WAS BORN

"Mom! There's a ghost in our house, and we can talk to it!" Maggie Fox was 14, and her sister Kate was 11, when they played a prank so clever, it changed history. In 1848, the American sisters told their mom and neighbor that a ghost had spoken to them by knocking on the floor.

"We'll prove it!" they said. "Ghost, how old is our neighbor?" The ghost pounded 33 times—it was correct. Maggie and Kate's mom and neighbor ran away in panic. The next thing the sisters knew, they were moving in with their older sister because their mom had sold the haunted house!

They told only their big sister, Leah, that the knocking was really an apple on a string. Leah didn't tell on them—instead, she joined in on the act! Soon, the three Fox sisters became world famous for communicating with the dead. More and more women started to claim they could do it too. They were called *mediums*, and they led meetings called *séances* in which they said the dead communicated through them. It became one of the world's fastest-growing religions: spiritualism. Millions of people believed.

Spiritualism was an unusual religion. There were no preachers, prayers, or rules. And it was no wonder so many people believed. Almost everyone involved had lost loved ones: Men died in wars, women died in childbirth, and children died of diseases all the time in the 1800s.

Later in life, in front of a crowd at a grand concert in New York, Maggie confessed that everything they did was only an act. "I could crack my toes inside my shoes," she said. "A great many people when they hear it believe that spirits are touching them." But spiritualism was too big to stop now. People said that bad ghosts made Maggie say those things, and they kept on believing.

THE EXPLORER

Elisha Kane was a famous Arctic explorer and scientist. He visited the Fox sisters, aiming to prove that they were fakes. But he fell in love instead! He married Maggie, and she promised to give up spiritualism.

THE BIRTH OF SPIRITUALISM

Millions attended séances in the early 1900s, hoping to speak to their dead loved ones through a medium. Adelaide Hermann, a very famous magician, thought mediums were cruel to trick people into believing they were speaking to the dead. She went to séances in disguise to try to expose the mediums' tricks!

SÉANCE

Spiritualists believed a séance required 12 men and women. Everyone gathered around a table, and the lights were dimmed.

TRICKS OF THE TRADE

Exactly how did some mediums fake their chats with the dead? Myth-busting magicians like Adelaide Hermann exposed some of their tricks. Here are the most common ones:

Ghosts were said to write messages in chalk, but mediums could write with their toes while no one was looking!

To fake an eerie voice when speaking through a horn, mediums put chemicals inside that fizzed and warbled.

When ghosts flew across the ceiling during a séance, Adelaide flashed a light: Sure enough, they were just papier-mâché ghosts on a string!

Did ghosts really protect mediums from flames? No, said Adelaide—they had fireproof chemicals on their hands.

Some mediums claimed a ghostly ooze called ectoplasm came out of them during a séance. But Adelaide discovered they had just swallowed cloth, then puked it up!

People thought "ghost portraits" proved ghosts existed. But really, it was just two photos copied onto one film.

THE LIJADU SISTERS

IDENTICAL TWINS CHANGED AFRICAN POP MUSIC FOREVER

Growing up in Nigeria, identical twins Taiwo and Kehinde *loved* music. The Lijadu sisters listened to music from Nigeria, from all over Africa, and from all over the world! Reggae, American blues, Afrobeat, rock and roll, they loved it all.

Taiwo and Kehinde weren't just twin sisters, they were also inseparable best friends. They began writing songs together while they were still children and quickly created their own unique sound. But the Lijadus had a problem—many people in Nigeria believed women didn't belong in the music business. The sisters knew they had something important to say, and they refused to give up. They believed their music was a way to change the world.

Writing songs about the problems they saw in their communities, the Lijadus spoke up for women's equality—and became some of the most popular musicians in Nigeria!

The Lijadus sang in three languages: English, Yoruba, and Ibo. Their songs combined the many different styles of music they loved. They always performed in matching outfits, and audiences were amazed at the complicated harmonies they created. When the sisters decided to move to the United States, many believed they would soon be as famous in North America as they were in Africa.

But something terrible happened. In 1996, Kehinde fell down a flight of stairs and was so badly hurt, doctors thought she might never walk again. The Lijadu sisters stopped performing and focused all their energy on helping Kehinde heal. The sisters studied herbal medicine and their Yoruba religion, and both became Yoruba priestesses. And then, after many years of hard work, Kehinde began to walk again! After so long away from the stage, the sisters began performing together once more. They lived happily together in their New York City apartment.

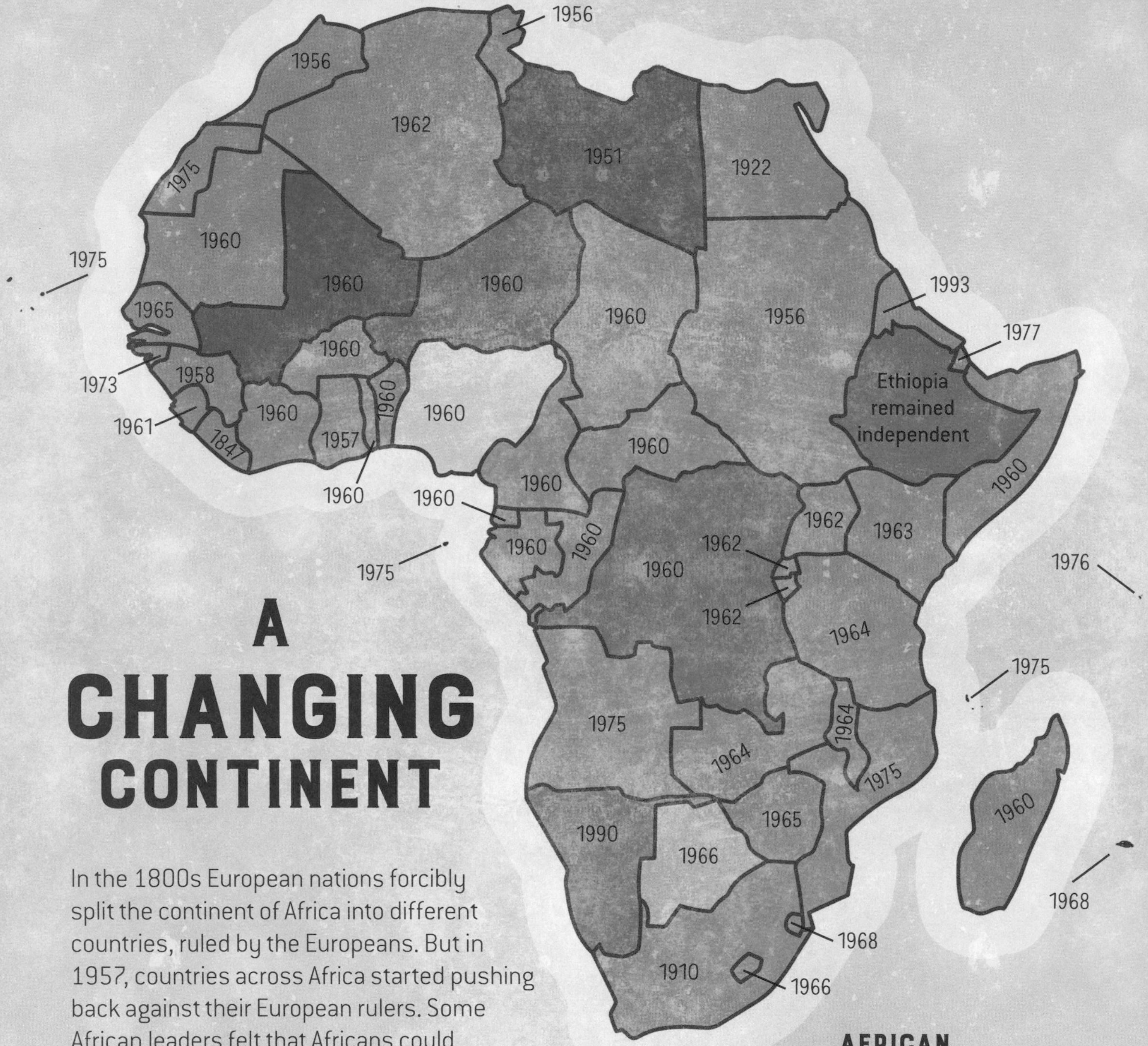

Map labels (dates of African independence):

1956 · 1956 · 1962 · 1951 · 1922 · 1975 · 1975 · 1960 · 1993 · 1965 · 1960 · 1960 · 1960 · 1956 · 1977 · 1960 · 1973 · 1958 · 1960 · 1960 · Ethiopia remained independent · 1961 · 1847 · 1957 · 1960 · 1960 · 1960 · 1960 · 1960 · 1960 · 1960 · 1960 · 1960 · 1960 · 1960 · 1962 · 1963 · 1960 · 1975 · 1960 · 1962 · 1976 · 1960 · 1962 · 1964 · 1975 · 1964 · 1964 · 1975 · 1960 · 1975 · 1990 · 1965 · 1968 · 1966 · 1968 · 1910 · 1966

A CHANGING CONTINENT

In the 1800s European nations forcibly split the continent of Africa into different countries, ruled by the Europeans. But in 1957, countries across Africa started pushing back against their European rulers. Some African leaders felt that Africans could achieve anything if they all worked together, so they started a movement called Pan-Africanism, celebrating everything Africans had in common. Music, food, stories, art, and sports brought Africans together. They even created a new winter holiday, Kwanzaa, to celebrate African culture.

AFRICAN INDEPENDENCE

In just over ten years, almost all African countries gained independence—the dates are in the map above. Sometimes it happened peacefully. Other times there was terrible bloodshed. European countries had controlled Africa for more than 100 years, but now Africans would build their own nations.

THE INFLUENCE OF MUSIC

Many people believe music is the best way to help people from different places understand one another. Try listening to some music from another country—does it help you imagine what life is like there? The Lijadus weren't the only pioneering singers from the continent of Africa. Here are a few other stars you can listen to.

ONYEKA ONWENU

Onyeka uses her music to try and make Nigeria—and the world—a more peaceful place. Her songs encourage people to be brave, be kind, and stand up for what they believe is right.

MIRIAM MAKEBA

Miriam grew up in South Africa when people were separated by race, in a system called apartheid. Her own government banned her from South Africa for protesting the laws! But her music crossed borders and became popular all over the world.

ANGÉLIQUE KIDJO

Angélique was a teenager in Benin while politicians kept musicians from doing anything new. Maybe that's why she loves combining musical styles from all over the world to create her own amazing sounds.

THE McDONAGH SISTERS

MOVIEMAKING TEAM ISABEL, PHYLLIS, AND PAULETTE McDONAGH WERE THE QUEENS OF AUSTRALIAN SILENT FILM

When John McDonagh died in 1920, his will left his three daughters $1,000 "to make a film." This gift probably surprised the neighbors, because making movies wasn't something women did in Australia. But in only a few years the sisters became the country's most famous—and only female—filmmaking team. Oldest sister Isabel was the star of their movies, Phyllis was producer and art director, and Paulette wrote and directed each film.

The sisters were a perfect team because they all shared the same style and vision. Their dramatic films were very different from the "outback adventures" other studios made—Isabel's acting was more realistic than the melodramatic, over-the-top style of the time, and it perfectly matched Paulette's directing and Phyllis's designs. Critics called their movies "dazzling" and audiences loved Isabel's unusual characters, who did everything from dancing on the beach to cracking safes. One of their movies even made the prime minister of Australia cry!

But as speaking films, or "talkies," took over the theaters, the McDonaghs struggled to keep up. They tried to add sound to their movies, but the effects were so awkward that the audience ended up laughing when they were meant to be sad. The sisters' filmmaking days were over, and they went their separate ways. Paulette stayed in Australia and made documentaries, Phyllis became a journalist in New Zealand, and Isabel launched a stage career in England. But even though their reign as "Cinema Queens" was short, the McDonaghs' movies are still praised as some of the best silent films ever made.

SILENT MOVIES

Because silent films are, well, silent, a musician in the theater improvised music for each scene. This made watching a movie with no sound much more exciting!

THE GILDED AGE

At the same time the McDonagh sisters were making silent films, countless new inventions were changing the lives of many people. This period at the start of the 1900s was called the "Gilded Age." What an exciting time to be alive! But was it all good news? When a thing is gilded, it's coated with a thin layer of shiny gold—so it looks like solid gold, but it might really be something nasty underneath.

MAKING STEEL

Steel is one of the strongest metals on Earth. When people figured out how to produce it on a large scale, everything changed. Workers now labored 12 hours a day, seven days a week! Skyscrapers, long bridges, railroads, and cars exist because of steel.

BIKE POWER

The invention of bicycles meant freedom, especially for women. For the first time, they could go fast and far, alone. Women's rights activist Susan B. Anthony said, "It has done more to [free] women than anything else in the world." Think of that next time you ride a bike!

LIGHT BULB

When Thomas Edison invented the light bulb, many people were wary of using it. They thought lamps full of burning oil were safer than the strange new thing called electricity!

CAMERA

Now photos are everywhere, but back then, seeing a photo was an amazing new thing. Cameras were large and heavy, with big glass plates. Most people could only afford one or two photos in their lifetime.

TELEPHONE

The telephone may have been the most amazing invention of the Gilded Age. Since the beginning of time, no one had ever been able to hear the voice of someone many miles away. But now you could!

MOVING IMAGE

Photos were amazing enough, but when people discovered how to make photos move, well, it seemed like magic. This was where the McDonagh sisters came in. Early movie cameras had noisy motors, like power tools—good thing the films were silent!

THE ROMANOV SISTERS

NOT EVERY PRINCESS GETS TO LIVE HAPPILY EVER AFTER

TSAR NICHOLAS II

Tsars had ruled Russia for 300 years when Nicholas II became emperor at the age of 26. But he ignored the poorest people in his empire, and he paid the ultimate price. The dynasty ended forever.

Tsar Nicholas and Tsarina Alexandra, the rulers of Russia, had five children: Olga, Tatiana, Maria, Anastasia, and their younger brother, Alexei. They were a very happy family. The girls loved climbing trees, sewing, taking photographs, and working in the garden together. As they grew up, the sisters dreamed of the exciting possibilities their lives might hold. But when the Russian Revolution began in 1917, Nicholas was forced to give up being emperor.

The family was held hostage by the Bolsheviks, a group of revolutionaries who believed Russia should be run by the people, not the rich elite. The former royal family were moved to different houses every few months. When they were allowed, the sisters tried to keep everyone's spirits up by playing the piano or singing. But 13-year-old Alexei was often ill, and as the guards became crueler, the family struggled to stay hopeful.

HOUSE ARREST

After their father was removed from the throne, the Romanovs were held captive in the Alexander Palace for months. The family were watched constantly by armed guards and couldn't leave their home.

After more than a year as prisoners, in July 1918, the family was taken to a small underground room. There, men from the secret police killed the entire family. The Bolsheviks wanted to keep the murders a secret, so they buried the bodies of the Romanovs in two shallow pits, hoping nobody would ever find them. Because of this, the true fate of the Romanovs remained a mystery until the last grave was finally discovered in 2007.

THE RUSSIAN REVOLUTION

For 300 years, the rich were *very* rich in Russia, and the poor were *very* poor. But in 1905, the poorest people stormed the royal palace, demanding that Tsar Nicholas II make things fairer. He promised he would. Twelve years went by, but nothing changed. So in 1917, an even bigger revolt—a revolution—ended the power of the tsars. The rebels dreamed of a new Russia, where the people ruled themselves.

REBEL HERO

Vladimir Lenin's big brother died trying to overthrow the tsar, and that made Vladimir fight even harder! He became a hero to the rebels, trying to build a Russia where everyone was truly equal. When he died, his body was preserved in a glass coffin so his people could always see and honor him. You can still visit Lenin today!

KARL MARX

People hoping for equality fought revolutions all over the world—not just in Russia. They were inspired by a writer named Karl Marx, who said that poor people needed to rise up and fight against the rich. Only when everyone is equal, he said, will we have a good, fair world.

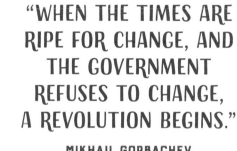

THE GREAT WAR

Russia was in the middle of fighting World War I when the revolution happened. WWI was seen as a horrible, deadly, pointless war. The people wanted to stop sending their sons to die in it. Rebel leaders said, "If we overthrow the tsar, we can exit the war!" And that's exactly what happened.

RASPUTIN

Some people believe an evil mystic named Grigori Rasputin controlled the minds of the tsar and his family, convincing them to act badly. Or is that just a way to excuse the royals for failing to help the poor?

> "WHEN THE TIMES ARE RIPE FOR CHANGE, AND THE GOVERNMENT REFUSES TO CHANGE, A REVOLUTION BEGINS."
>
> **MIKHAIL GORBACHEV
> RUSSIAN LEADER, 1985-1991**

THE PRETENDERS

After the royal family was murdered, rumors spread that Princess Anastasia was still alive! Soon, different women claimed they were Anastasia. The most famous "pretender" was Anna Anderson, who knew many amazing things only the real Anastasia would know. Royal relatives said she looked and talked just the same. Now we know that Anastasia did die with her family in 1918, but some people still believe the stories.

LUM GUEY & HOW JIU

WITH ONE TERRIBLE TWIST OF FATE, TWO CHINESE SISTERS' LIVES CHANGED FOREVER

PAPER FAMILIES

Because American laws banned Chinese immigrants, many came using "paper names." These were made-up identities that let immigrants like How Jiu start new lives. As a "paper daughter," How Jiu had to memorize every possible fact about her new "family" to avoid getting caught!

ANGEL ISLAND

Chinese immigrants hoping to move to the United States first arrived at Angel Island, off the coast of San Francisco. Here guards questioned everyone about their identity. Interviews often took months, trick questions were common, and one mistake would get you sent back to China.

In 1928, How Jiu boarded a ship bound for the United States and a brand-new life. The only problem? How Jiu didn't exist.

In a village in southeast China lived two sisters, Lum Guey and Lum Wun Hoy. The sisters were always together, playing in the nearby orange groves or raising pigs for their father's butcher shop. But a brutal war raged across China, and their parents were afraid. "It's not safe for you here anymore," they told Lum Guey. "We have bought you a trip to California." The parents loved both daughters, but they could only afford one ticket. The USA wouldn't allow Chinese immigrants into the country, so an American family agreed to pretend Lum Guey was their daughter—How Jiu. Lum Guey was excited to go but sad to leave her sister behind.

Meanwhile, bandits roamed the hills of Guangzhou, where the sisters lived. When the bandits couldn't find anything to steal, they stole people instead. To the family's horror, they stole Lum Guey! The kidnappers demanded a ransom, but it would take time to raise the money—and the ship to the USA was about to set sail. There was only one thing they could do: Lum Wun Hoy took her sister's place.

In that fateful moment, the sisters traded futures. Lum Wun Hoy sailed off to California to become "How Jiu," while Lum Guey stayed in China. How Jiu married, had children, and traveled the world. Lum Guey, who was eventually freed by the bandits, lived in their tiny village her whole life. What do you think the sisters thought about how things turned out?

A TALE OF TWO COUNTRIES

Earth's largest and deepest ocean separates China and the United States. Many thousands of years ago, the very first humans to live in North America traveled there from Asia. But for most of modern history, very few people ever crossed the vast Pacific Ocean. All that changed in the 1800s, when lots of Chinese people decided to try their luck in the USA—a country that seemed to be a rising star. Just like How Jiu, thousands boarded ships to seek the unknown. Can you imagine sailing off to a completely new life?

ANGEL ISLAND

CHINESE CIVIL WAR

China fought wars with many other countries in the 1800s, making life unstable and frightening. By How Jiu's time in the 1920s, China was at war with itself—what's known as a civil war. Both sides claimed they were fighting for a righteous cause and that they knew the best way to rebuild China for the people. The war dragged on for more than 20 years.

MELTING POT

The USA seemed like the place where dreams came true in the 1800s. Immigrants came from all over the world hoping for a new life. On the East Coast they arrived at Ellis Island in New York, while on the West Coast new visitors first had to go to Angel Island—just like How Jiu. In just one American neighborhood you could hear many languages, smell and taste foods from all over the world, and see so much diversity that you would understand why they called the USA a "melting pot."

ELLIS ISLAND

NO CHINESE!

YOU'RE NOT WELCOME

GO HOME

CHINESE EXCLUSION ACT

A strange thing happened while people were coming to the USA from all over the world. Large groups of workers—most of them immigrants themselves—decided that Chinese people threatened their jobs and their dreams. They convinced the US government to pass a law banning Chinese people from coming to the USA.

MAO ZEDONG

CULTURAL REVOLUTION

Mao Zedong and his Communist Party won the Chinese Civil War. Once in power, they decided that old traditions had to be crushed to make way for the future. Young people were fired up by the motto: "Smash the old world, build a new one." And they did just that.

SAMARKAND

JERUSALEM

SARAH & SONIA CHAMINOV

TWO YOUNG SISTERS TOOK A DEATH-DEFYING JOURNEY IN SEARCH OF A SAFE PLACE TO LIVE

Sarah and Sonia Chaminov's family had lived in the ancient city of Samarkand for generations. But by 1932, chaos from the Russian Revolution was making it too dangerous for a Jewish family to stay in Uzbekistan. How do you escape when the government says you're not allowed to leave? You sneak out on a camel caravan!

The Chaminovs loaded a few precious possessions into packs and paid a group of traveling merchants to smuggle them, along with a few other families, over 4,400 miles (7,100 km) to Jerusalem. Every day they risked being discovered by soldiers or attacked by robbers, and almost everyone was on foot. Fourteen-year-old Sarah walked over high mountains and through desert sands, which sometimes came up to her knees, across six countries! But those who were too old or too young to walk rode on camels. Each saddle held two adults balanced on either side of the camel's body, and two-year-old Sonia sat on her grandmother's lap.

The woman sharing their grandmother's camel kept complaining that Sonia's extra weight was shifting the saddle to one side. Sarah had heard awful stories of the babies of refugees being smothered when their crying put the caravan in danger. She was terrified that if the other woman kept grumbling, the smugglers would make them abandon Sonia in the desert. So for six months, she walked right alongside Sonia's camel, pushing the saddle up each time it slipped. Sarah's dedication kept her sister safe all the way to Jerusalem.

LIFE AS A REFUGEE

Sometimes when people aren't safe in their own countries—because of things like wars, pollution, natural disasters, racism, or violence—they have to leave without much warning. People searching for a new place to live are called refugees. The Chaminovs were lucky to find a safe new home after their long journey. But many refugees around the world spend years, sometimes even the rest of their lives, looking for a place to call home.

TOUGH JOURNEYS

Refugees often have to travel long distances to find safety. Whether they go by boat, train, truck, camel, or their own two feet, searching for a new home can be difficult and dangerous.

PLACES TO STAY

Many refugees end up living in camps—makeshift cities of tents or trailers. These camps are meant to be temporary, but some refugees get stuck there so long, they can't remember living anywhere else.

SCHOOLTIME

Every child deserves a safe place to learn. So some refugee camps build temporary schools. Students can study reading, writing, music, mathematics, and sometimes even a new language so they can communicate in their new home.

"A REFUGEE IS SOMEONE WHO SURVIVED AND WHO CAN CREATE THE FUTURE."

AMELA KOLUDER

A WARM WELCOME

Every day, kind people around the world work together to welcome refugees into their communities. In their new countries, in safe homes, and with new friends, refugee families are starting the next chapter of their lives.

TRUUS & FREDDIE OVERSTEEGEN

HOW FAR WOULD YOU GO TO SAVE SOMEONE ELSE'S LIFE?

When German president Adolf Hitler began threatening Jewish people at the beginning of World War II, thousands of families fled the country. When many of those refugees arrived in the Netherlands, the Oversteegen family wanted to help. Sisters Truus and Freddie gave up their own beds to hide a Jewish family with nowhere to go. And when Hitler's Nazi army invaded the Netherlands a few years later, the sisters believed they had to choose: either decide to fight back, or allow innocent people to die.

Truus, who was 16, and 14-year-old Freddie joined the Dutch Resistance, a secret group trying to protect Jewish people and disrupt the German army's plans. They knew Nazis always underestimated what girls could accomplish. So the sisters used that to their advantage and became two of the deadliest assassins in the country.

In order to save innocent lives, the sisters killed Nazi soldiers or Dutch traitors who were murdering Jewish people. Working together, or with a friend named Hannie Schaft, the sisters would ride past their "target" on bicycles, then shoot them. Sometimes they would invite enemy soldiers on a walk in the woods—before assassinating them. The sisters hated killing, but they knew they were saving hundreds of lives. So they kept doing it. When the war finally ended, Truus became an artist and Freddie raised three children, but both were haunted by the past. How might their lives have been different if they had never had to make such a terrible choice?

SAVING CHILDREN

Because girls could travel with young children without anyone getting suspicious, Truus and Hannie Schaft often helped smuggle Jewish children to safe houses in other cities, or even to other countries.

SPY WORK

Truus and Freddie helped the Dutch Resistance in other ways too. They stole military information, burned down buildings, and even helped blow up Nazi trains!

THE WORLD AT WAR

ADOLF HITLER

The people of Germany had suffered for years after their government collapsed following World War I. So when a man named Adolf Hitler promised he could fix everything, they put him in charge. He built an army and started the war.

Almost every country in the world was sucked into World War II. That's one reason the historian Sir Max Hastings called it "the biggest event in the history of the world." At the heart of the war was a global fight over which type of government could build the greatest country. In the end, 60 million people died. It's hard to believe something so awful could happen—and so recently. Now, we carefully study what happened, so we can make sure it never happens again.

WAR IN ASIA

Japan built a massive empire, attacking China, then Burma, Indonesia, the Philippines, and India. Meanwhile Europe and the United States claimed those South East Asian countries belonged to them. So 20 countries fought on land and sea for control of Asia and the Pacific Ocean.

WOMEN SOLDIERS

Women had very different war experiences depending on where they lived. The Philippines, China, and the USSR (now Russia) welcomed women as brave, strong soldiers. Some of the greatest snipers—soldiers who could hit a target from far, far away—were women.

CONCENTRATION CAMPS

Hitler said that to build a stronger nation, Germany had to kill entire groups of people, including Jews, Slavs, and people with disabilities. And his people believed him. Six million men, women, and children were forced into concentration camps, then killed. It's so shocking, we are still trying to understand how it ever happened.

TOTAL WAR

World War II wasn't just fought between soldiers on battlefields: *Everyone* was involved. The luckiest people only had to ration, or limit, what food they ate, as supplies were so low. Others had to defend their home from invaders, or hide in bunkers while bombs destroyed their cities. This is known as "total war."

FACTORY WORK

In places like Britain, the United States, Australia, and Germany, women were asked to help in other ways. They worked in mines and factories, repaired planes and tanks, and farmed in clever new ways to produce enough food for their people.

MARIA & MARJORIE TALLCHIEF

RUSSIAN BALLERINAS RULED THE STAGE—UNTIL TWO NATIVE AMERICAN SISTERS CHANGED BALLET FOREVER

BALLET SCHOOL

The Tallchief sisters originally hoped to be in movies. They studied Spanish dancing, tap, and acrobatics with Hollywood choreographer Ernest Belcher before deciding to focus on ballet.

Attending a performance of *The Nutcracker* is a yearly tradition for millions of families. But how did it become the most popular ballet in the world? It's all because of the amazing Maria Tallchief.

Maria and Marjorie Tallchief grew up on the Osage Reservation and started dance lessons when they were only three years old. When their parents realized the girls were especially talented, they moved from Oklahoma to California to help them succeed. After studying with excellent teachers, the sisters joined world-famous dance companies. Many people pushed the Tallchiefs to hide their Native American identity. Some suggested changing their name to the Russian-sounding "Tolchieva"—Russian ballerinas were supposed to be the best—but the sisters refused. They were proud to be Osage and wouldn't hide it!

When Maria joined New York City Ballet in 1948, she became the USA's first "homegrown" prima ballerina. Then Marjorie became the first Native American prima ballerina with the Paris Opera. The sisters weren't just good—they were two of the best dancers in the world. Marjorie was able to dance many different styles, and she starred with famous companies worldwide. Maria was so strong and graceful that even other famous dancers couldn't perform her complex choreography.

One of Maria's performances was so incredible, it changed ballet history. For decades *The Nutcracker* was barely performed. But Maria's dancing as the Sugar Plum Fairy was so magical, it helped make the ballet a holiday tradition all around the world.

THE FIVE MOONS

From the 1930s to the 1950s, five of the best ballerinas in the world were Native American—and they were all from Oklahoma! Yvonne Chouteau, Rosella Hightower, Moscelyne Larkin, Maria Tallchief, and Marjorie Tallchief all rose to fame at about the same time.

TLINGIT

HAIDA

CHIPEWYAN

CREE

NUU-CHAH-NULTH

MI'KMAQ

CHINOOK

BLACKFEET

ASSINIBOINE

ANISHINAABE

ABENAKI

HURON

MANDAN

IROQUOIS

SHOSHONE

SIOUX

DELAWARE

SHAWNEE

CHUMASH

POWHATAN

PAWNEE

NAVAJO

OSAGE

PUEBLO   COMANCHE

CHEROKEE

APACHE

YAQUI

CADDO   CHOCTAW   CREEK

NATCHEZ

TIMUCUA

CALUSA

MAYA

PURÉPECHA

DIFFERENT TRIBES

Untold numbers of Native American tribes spread across North America. This map shows the locations of some tribes—but it is greatly simplified and doesn't show all of them. Like humans everywhere, Native Americans befriended one another, fought one another, saved one another, and killed one another. Some think that because Native Americans were never unified as one, they had no chance of resisting the European conquerors.

NATIVE AMERICAN LIFE

When European sailor Christopher Columbus first set foot in North America in 1492, 60 million people lived in the Americas. Their ancestors had come from Asia 20,000 years ago. The arrival of the Europeans saw Native Americans wiped out in large numbers—through conflict and European diseases. Life for many Native Americans has been a struggle ever since.

BOARDING SCHOOLS

Starting in 1860, the US government said Native Americans would be better off if they lived like white people. They built boarding schools for Native American kids, with the motto "kill the Indian to save the man." For 100 years, the schools tried to erase children's culture, punishing them for speaking their native language or growing their hair long.

DIFFERENT LIFESTYLES

The 10% of Native Americans who survived the European conquest adapted in lots of ways. Many moved to reservations, special land where they aimed to live in traditional ways. Reservations were technically independent nations, but the US government only allotted them the worst land. Some Native Americans became wealthy farmers, living just like white Americans. Members of Maria and Marjorie's tribe—the Osage— briefly became very wealthy when oil was found on their land.

INDIAN CITIZENSHIP ACT

Previous US laws took land from Native Americans if they weren't "using it" for farming. But by the 1920s, things finally started to change. An act was passed that at last made Native people US citizens, and in 1928, two million acres were returned to Native tribes.

RAFAEL TRUJILLO

Known by the nickname *el Jefe*—
"the boss"—Rafael Trujillo used
money, terror, and torture to rule
the Dominican Republic for
31 years.

DEDÉ MIRABAL

The fourth Mirabal sister wasn't
involved in the Butterflies' work
and wasn't killed with them. But
by keeping their story alive, she
helped inspire the revolution that
finally defeated Trujillo.

THE MIRABAL SISTERS

DECADES AFTER THEY DIED, THE MIRABAL SISTERS ARE STILL CELEBRATED AS HEROES OF THE DOMINICAN REPUBLIC

Growing up under their country's brutal dictator Rafael Trujillo,
sisters Patria, Minerva, and María Teresa Mirabal didn't just hope
for things to change, they formed a secret resistance group!
They called themselves *Las Mariposas*—the Butterflies.
Working together, the Mirabal sisters built weapons to fight
Trujillo's secret police, published the truth about the many
people he had killed, and helped show everyone how
dangerous the dictator of the Caribbean nation really was.

Of course, this made Trujillo furious. He kept having the sisters
arrested—even tortured—to try to stop them. When the sisters
still refused to give in, he even locked up their families to force
them to back down. But the Mirabals would not be silenced.
They were determined to stand up to the tyrant.

Then in 1960, the sisters were driving home after visiting their
husbands in prison. They were stopped by Trujillo's secret
police, who murdered all three women. Then the men put the
Mirabals back in the sisters' jeep and sent it over a cliff. They
were trying to make the killings look like an accident, but
everyone knew what had really happened.

People were so horrified by the assassination of the Mirabal
sisters that things in the country finally started to change. The
people's anger against Trujillo grew so strong that six months
after the murders, Trujillo himself was assassinated. And in the
Dominican Republic today, the Butterflies are honored for their
courage and for helping to bring freedom to the country.

On this map the countries in orange were on team USA, and the countries in red were team USSR.

DOMINICAN REPUBLIC

TWO SIDES

The two main rivals in the Cold War were the United States of America (USA) and the United Soviet Socialist Republic (USSR). Each country was convinced that its way of life was the best, and that its enemies were evil. Most countries in the world were forced to choose a side!

THE COLD WAR

The Mirabal sisters lived through one episode in a huge global war. Starting in 1945, Earth teetered on the brink of total destruction due to the emergence of atomic weapons. People feared enemies would drop bombs from the sky at any time. Kids had bomb drills at school, and towns built huge sirens. But the bombs never came. Now, we call it the Cold War, because the main rival nations never actually battled. Looking back, it's clear that around the world, common people wanted peace more than war.

ATOMIC WEAPONS

The USA invented an unimaginably powerful bomb that worked by splitting apart atoms—the tiny building blocks of life. When the USSR saw it, they built lots of their own. Soon countries across the world had atomic missiles aimed at their enemies.

VIETNAM WAR

The USA and USSR often meddled in other countries' wars. In South East Asia, Vietnam chose team USSR. But the American president believed many Vietnamese secretly wanted team USA, so he sent an army. The resulting war was devastating.

BERLIN WALL

The German city of Berlin was half team USSR, half team USA! A massive wall was built down the middle of the city, and guards kept people separate. But by 1989, the USSR was breaking apart. Young people tore down the wall and celebrated. The world watched in awe: The Cold War was over.

NOV. 25

INTERNATIONAL DAY FOR THE ELIMINATION OF VIOLENCE AGAINST WOMEN

UN DECLARATION

The Mirabal sisters were killed on November 25. Now, every 25th of November is dedicated to ending violence against women. The United Nations declared the special day because in history, men have had too much power over women. Today we are trying to undo that!

QUEEN ELIZABETH

WHAT'S IT LIKE TO BE THE LITTLE SISTER OF THE MOST FAMOUS WOMAN IN THE WORLD?

Elizabeth Windsor was four years old when her sister, Margaret, was born. As children of the British royal family, the sisters didn't have many playmates, so they spent almost all their time together. Their personalities were very different. While Elizabeth was quiet and calm, Margaret could be unpredictable and fiery. The family was a happy one, and the girls loved riding horses, studying with their governess, and playing in the garden with their parents. Then, when Elizabeth was ten years old, their father Prince Albert unexpectedly became king!

The sisters' lives were about to change— and the age difference that had never mattered before now meant that Elizabeth was destined to become queen, and Margaret was not.

RADIO

In 1940, the princesses gave their very first radio broadcast, speaking to children around the world who were living through World War II.

& PRINCESS MARGARET

Nevertheless, the sisters stayed close, even after Elizabeth took the throne in 1953. Margaret was one of the only people allowed to telephone the queen, and they chatted almost every day. But when a big sister has that much power, things get complicated. Elizabeth had the final say on big choices in Margaret's life, such as who she could marry or where she could live, and Margaret sometimes resented that control. And while Elizabeth took her royal responsibilities very seriously, Margaret was usually more interested in having fun than in "behaving properly." This sometimes caused big problems for the royal family.

Through it all, the sisters remained fiercely loyal to one another. When Princess Margaret died in 2002, Elizabeth cried at her funeral—something she almost never did in public. Though the relationship may not always have been easy, these royal sisters were friends to the very end.

REBEL

Princess Margaret's romantic relationships, wild parties, and scandalous behavior often caused trouble for the royal family.

VENUS & SERENA WILLIAMS

THESE TENNIS SUPERSTARS ALWAYS SUPPORT EACH OTHER, EVEN WHEN THEY HAVE TO GO HEAD-TO-HEAD!

The first time eight-year-old Venus Williams faced her little sister in a competition, it was because Serena had pulled a sneaky trick. Though the American sisters had been playing tennis for years, their dad thought seven-year-old Serena was too young to compete. But Serena wouldn't take no for an answer—she secretly filled out an entry form and mailed it in herself. While the family cheered for Venus, Serena quietly disappeared to play her match—and she won! She expected her father to be angry, but instead he was proud. He gave her tips to win her next match, and sure enough she did. All day long, Venus and Serena won, and won, and won, until they faced each other in the final. Venus defeated her sister easily that day, but Serena had shown she could definitely compete on the courts.

As the girls improved, they needed better coaching than their dad could give them. A famous coach offered to teach the sisters for free, but they had to move to Florida. It was a big decision, but their parents knew the girls had something special. So they went, and Venus and Serena went from great to incredible! Soon everyone could see they were going to be superstars. Each sister won a Grand Slam (which means one of the four top tennis competitions in the world) before her 20th birthday. And after a lifetime playing together, it's no surprise that as a doubles team the Williams sisters are practically unstoppable—they've won 14 Grand Slams together!

PRODIGIES

Venus and Serena's dad started teaching them to play tennis at four years old. After ten years of practicing for hours every day, they each started playing professionally at 14.

TROPHIES

Together, the Williams sisters have won more than 120 major tennis titles and three Olympic gold medals.

THE MALIK SISTERS

CLIMBING EARTH'S HIGHEST PEAKS, THE MALIK TWINS ARE INSPIRING GIRLS AROUND THE WORLD

Have you ever been on a really long hike? I mean really, *really* long? The Malik sisters have probably gone farther—together they climbed the highest mountain in the world when they were only 21 years old! Twin sisters Tashi and Nungshi Malik were born in Haryana, India, in 1991, and they've been inseparable ever since. Growing up, the sisters loved playing basketball, badminton, and hockey. But it was at the age of 18 that they discovered their true passion: mountaineering.

After climbing their first mountain, the Maliks were hooked, and they wanted to be the very best. They climbed many of the most famous mountains in Asia, but when they decided to tackle "the big one," Mount Everest, their mother was worried. She knew how dangerous that climb was. The sisters were determined to conquer the world's highest peak, and it wasn't long before they did!

After they returned from Everest, the Maliks thought their mountaineering days might be over. But when they noticed how often girls are discouraged from following their own dreams, Tashi and Nungshi decided to continue climbing. They wanted to prove that women can do anything men can! Now the Malik sisters encourage girls everywhere to overcome the "invisible mountains" that keep them from reaching their goals.

SEVEN SUMMITS

In 2015, the Malik sisters became the youngest people (and only siblings) ever to complete the "Explorer's Grand Slam." This meant climbing the highest peak on every continent and trekking to both the North and South Poles. They were only 23 years old!

"OUR MOTHER GAVE US THREE OPTIONS—
CLIMB EVEREST, GET MARRIED, OR STUDY
ABROAD. IT WAS AN EASY CHOICE."

TASHI MALIK

A WORLD FULL OF
SISTERS

IN THIS BOOK WE'VE MET MANY DIFFERENT KINDS OF SISTERS. ALL OF THEM CHANGED THE WORLD.

Sometimes, sisters competing against one another spurred them on to greatness, like the Williams sisters and the Brontës. Other times, competition destroyed them, like Cleopatra and Arsinoë, Anna and Brita Zippel, or the Begum princesses.

But we've also seen sisters who used their opposite-ness to their advantage! If you draw from one another's specific strengths, you can help each other be brave, like the Nakano, Trung, and Oversteegen sisters. Or you can combine your different skills to build a great team, like the McDonagh, Hyers, and Fox sisters.

We've also seen plenty of women who played incredibly important roles in history: Olympe de Gouges, Elizabeth Tudor, and Caroline Herschel all changed the course of the future. But their own sisters were always at the heart of each of their stories.

Destiny seems to put our sisters into our lives. But after that—who knows? Perhaps we'll spend our lives side by side, like Tashi and Nungshi Malik or the Lijadu sisters. Or maybe fate will fling us in very different directions, like How Jiu and Lum Guey or the Mongol Khatun.

But whether they are near or far, allies or enemies—for better or for worse, as long as there are sisters, they will continue to be a powerful force in the human story.

ABOUT THE AUTHORS

Katie Nelson and Olivia Meikle are professors, podcasters—and sisters! Their first joint venture was a speculative enterprise where Katie (age 7) attempted to dig a hole to China, and Olivia (age 11) built a hospital for all the worms that came out of the hole. The project went so well that they've enjoyed working together ever since. Together they host the popular *What'sHerName* history podcast. These days they teach History (Katie) and Women's Studies (Olivia) on opposite sides of the Rocky Mountains. Between them, Katie and Olivia have two husbands, five kids, two parakeets, one schnauzer, and one hermit crab. Their other sister, Mera MacKendrick, did the illustrations on the right!

KATIE

OLIVIA

THE ILLUSTRATORS

GLOSSARY

Alchemist
Someone who attempts to turn normal metals into gold.

Apartheid
A system of racial oppression in South Africa in the second half of the 20th century.

Armada
A fleet of ships, particularly one that fights at sea. For example, the Spanish Armada.

Astronomer
Someone who studies space.

Astronomy
The study of space.

Bolshevik
A member of the Russian political movement that overthrew the Tsar in the Russian Revolution of 1917.

Catholicism
A branch of the Christian church, led by the Pope.

Civil war
A war that takes place between two or more sides within the same country.

Cold War
A war that took place from 1947 to 1991 between the USA and the USSR, characterized by a lack of direct fighting between the two superpowers (hence "Cold").

Colony
A territory ruled by another country.

Comet
An icy and rocky object that travels through space.

Communism
A political system that aims to spread power among the people, popular in many countries in the 20th century.

Cuneiform
An early form of writing devised by ancient Mesopotamians.

Dictator
A ruler with total power who leads a country by force.

Empire
A collection of countries or territories ruled by one person—the emperor. For example, the Roman Empire.

The Enlightenment
A period of European history in the 1700s characterized by an emphasis on learning.

Garum
A fermented fish sauce popular in ancient Rome.

Immigrant
Someone who moves from one country to another.

Industrial Revolution
A period of the 18th and 19th centuries characterized by the mass production of goods in factories and the invention of railroads and steamships.

Liberty
The pursuit of freedom.

Madrassa
An Islamic school.

Maya
A group of people who originated in Central America. The Maya are famous for their incredible temples, calendars, and art.

Medium
Someone who claims to be able to communicate with the dead.

Mesopotamia
An area in the Middle East that saw the rise of some of the first major civilizations, as well as the development of writing.

The Middle Ages
A period of European history that took place from the 5th century to the 15th century. Also known as the Medieval period. It was a time of kings and queens, castles, and exploration.

Mosque
An Islamic place of worship.

Pharaoh
The name for the kings of ancient Egypt.

Philosopher
Someone who studies the meaning of things.

Plantation
A large farm.

Polynesia
An area of the Pacific Ocean made up of lots of islands.

Porcelain
A form of pottery that emerged in China.

Printing press
A 15th-century invention that enabled books to be printed much more quickly and on a greater scale than before.

Protestantism
A branch of the Christian church that split from Catholicism in the Reformation of the 16th century.

Racism
The act of treating someone unfairly based on the color of their skin or where they come from.

Refugee
Someone, often a victim of war or famine, who seeks safety in a new country.

Republic
A system of government where the people elect officials to represent them (as opposed to an empire where one person rules over all).

Revolution
A rebellion against the ruling forces of a country.

Samurai
The historical ruling warrior class of Japan.

Scholar
Someone who studies a particular subject.

Séance
A gathering, led by a medium, where people try to communicate with the dead.

The Silk Road
An ancient trade route running from China in the east to Europe in the west, along which goods such as silk, spices, and porcelain were traded.

Slave
Someone owned by another human and forced to do things against their will.

Spiritualism
A religion that believes it is possible to communicate with the dead.

The Stone Age
An early period of human history characterized by the use of stone tools.

Suffragette
Someone who fought for women to have the same rights to vote as men.

Superpower
The name for an extremely powerful country—usually used in reference to the USA and USSR in the 20th century.

Tang Dynasty
The ruling family of ancient China in the years 618 CE to 907 CE.

Tsar
King of Russia.

The Tudors
The ruling family of England from 1485 until 1603. Rulers included Henry VIII and Elizabeth I.

INDEX

This has been a

NEON SQUID

production

To our sister, Meredith

Authors: Katie Nelson and Olivia Meikle
US Editor: Allison Singer

The authors would like to thank:

Irit Namatinya for photos, translations, and information on the Chaminov sisters; Miao Xiaojing for consultation and translation on the Song sisters pages; Ade Modile for consultation and translation on the Lijadu sisters pages; and Jill Au and Lena Fong for photos and information on How Jiu and Lum Guey.

Kid editors: Abby Clark, Elizabeth Gill, Vivienne Gill, Kaitley Jones, Gabriel Stoddard Salisbury, Liliana Thorley, Claire Warby, James Warby

Neon Squid would like to thank:

Darren Parry for reviewing the pages about the Tallchief sisters; Georgina Coles for proofreading; and Anna Lord for compiling the index.

This book is dedicated to our sisters: Hannah, Izzie, Rose, and Alannah.

Copyright © 2022 St. Martin's Press
120 Broadway, New York, NY 10271

Created for St. Martin's Press
by Neon Squid
The Stables, 4 Crinan Street,
London, N1 9XW

EU representative:
Macmillan Publishers Ireland Ltd,
1st Floor, The Liffey Trust Centre,
117-126 Sheriff Street Upper,
Dublin 1, D01 YC43

10 9 8 7 6 5 4 3 2 1

The rights of Katie Nelson and Olivia Meikle to be identified as the authors of this work has been asserted in accordance with the Copyright, Designs and Patents Act, 1988.

Library of Congress Cataloging-in-Publication Data is available.

Printed and bound by Vivar Printing in Malaysia.

ISBN: 978-1-684-49200-8

Published in February 2022.

www.neonsquidbooks.com